Stephanie mai

The Hound of t

and other Sherlo

The Hound of the Baskervilles

and other Sherlock Holmes plays

Plays by
Michael & Mollie Hardwick
from stories by
Sir Arthur Conan Doyle

John Murray

© Michael and Mollie Hardwick 1982

First published 1982
by John Murray (Publishers) Ltd
50 Albemarle Street, London W1X 4BD

Printed in Great Britain by
Martin's Printing Works, Berwick-upon-Tweed

British Library Cataloguing in Publication Data

Hardwick, Michael
The hound of the Baskervilles and other Sherlock Holmes plays.
1.   College and school drama
2.   One-set plays, English
3.   English drama—20th century
I. Title   II. Hardwick, Mollie
822'.041'08   PN6120.A4

ISBN 0-7195-3997-8

FOREWORD

As you pick up this book and look through it, you may find
yourself wondering: 'Why does the play mentioned in the
title, *The Hound of the Baskervilles*, come not at the beginning
but in the middle of this book, sandwiched between two
others?'

There is a good reason for this. The plays are in fact in the
'right' order, and they form a sequence without parallel in
literature.

If Arthur Conan Doyle had had his way, *The Final Problem*
would have wholly lived up to its title and been the last
Sherlock Holmes story he ever wrote, thus depriving us of
more than half the sixty which make up the canon. He
regarded these detective stories as inconsequential trifles
compared with his immensely detailed historical novels. He
had twice tried to turn his back on Holmes, but been dis-
suaded. But in December 1893 his ardent readers of the
Strand Magazine froze in shock on opening the page at Sidney
Paget's breathtaking illustration of their hero and his arch-
enemy, Professor Moriarty, overbalancing in their struggle
to the death on the brink of the precipitous Reichenbach
Falls.

'You beast!' a lady wrote to the author, who had so
callously killed off the fictional being who had been more real
to her than any from true history. Some City of London
clerks turned up for work wearing black mourning bands on
their sober sleeves. It was waggishly done, no doubt, but the
reading public felt genuine resentment that Holmes's
creator had selfishly decreed that they should have no more
of him. Their feeling can only be equated with that of today's

mass television audience when a favourite soap opera character is dramatically 'written out' of the series.

The Holmes stories were far from soap opera, however. The public sensed it, even if Conan Doyle did not. It was a classic instance of an author's not recognising where his unique genius lay; and, paradoxically, these *were* historical tales, potently evoking their period for all time. Personal tragedies and his preoccupation with the South African War and other grave public affairs had added to his seriousness of mind, though, and all efforts to persuade him to bring Holmes back were rebuffed.

After eight years there came at last a dawning of hope. In 1901 the *Strand* announced a brand new Sherlock Holmes adventure, and proceeded to run *The Hound of the Baskervilles* in nine monthly parts. Its author was still not conceding anything. It was only while working out this mystery of a spectral hound menacing the heirs to a remote Dartmoor estate that he realised how much it needed the genius of Holmes to solve it, and Dr Watson as eye-witness reporter. The difficulty that Holmes was purportedly dead was overcome by stating that the case had been an earlier one, hitherto unchronicled.

Following the death cries of the Hound, silence fell again. It was not until October 1903, following an approach by an American publisher which even Arthur Conan Doyle could not resist, that Holmes was restored to the land of the living, in a way which caused Watson to faint 'for the first and the last time in my life'. He titled his account *The Empty House;* and the reading public, in its joy, mobbed the bookstalls in a stampede that is inconceivable today.

How was Holmes brought back to life? You may hear him explain it himself in this volume, and it proves to be by no means one of those 'with one mighty bound he was free' cheats. Consider the evidence.

In *The Final Problem* Holmes's premonition is that

Moriarty is about to catch up with him at last. Watson is lured away by a trick, and returns to find the evidence of the fight to the death, ending his narrative with the seemingly final statement that both had perished.

Yet, Holmes is never *seen* to be dead. Had he been shot, or stabbed, or run over by a London horse-omnibus driven by one of Moriarty's gang, it would all have been so different. We do not suggest that Conan Doyle deliberately kept open a means of bringing him back, should he ever need the money. He was not that kind of writer. Our theory is that something instinctive stopped him short of irreversible finality. Vivid fictional characters have a way of dictating their own destinies, positively refusing to let their lives or deaths be manipulated to fit a preconceived plot. We think this was such a case, and this sequence of plays shows it working out.

The method of dramatisation we have used differs in each of the three instances. *The Final Problem* is a story told well after the events by a heavy-hearted Watson, the only person to have known most of the details. This intensely personal recollection is unsuited to being acted on the stage, though it works excellently on radio as a narrative interspersed with illustrative scenes, which is the way we have presented it here.

The Hound of the Baskervilles ideally calls for cameras, great space, stirring effects, and, above all, the culminating spectacle of the Hound launching itself at us in fearsome close-up, with burning jowls and unearthly cry. It has often been filmed, and it, too, works impressively on radio, especially if one cuts out the rather tedious and complicating sub-plot about the precise way Sir Charles Baskerville was lured to his death. We have left this element out of our version, and because what remains is still a long story, with Holmes off the scene for much of it, we have taken a pretty free hand with both action and dialogue, in a way not intended for staging.

The Empty House, by contrast, is presented in an acting version. It is an economical story, with few characters and sets, depending almost wholly on the joyous revelation of Holmes's 'return from the dead', his explanation of how he had survived and why he has waited three years before letting his grieving friend know, and then the dramatic climax of Colonel Sebastian Moran's attempt to consign him to the grave in a way from which there could be no coming back.

It includes much of that Holmes-Watson interplay which is the life-spirit of the Sherlock Holmes stories, and has many often-quoted lines. Therefore, we have stuck as closely to the original dialogue as possible, offering what should prove to be a notable challenge to the actors considered good enough to be cast as the immortal pair.

Michael & Mollie Hardwick

CONTENTS

THE FINAL PROBLEM

Characters in order of appearance:

DR WATSON

SHERLOCK HOLMES

PROFESSOR MORIARTY: (middle-aged; oily and precise)

PETER STEILER: (middle-aged; heavy accent)

SWISS YOUTH

THE FINAL PROBLEM

WATSON [*narrating*] : After my marriage and my subsequent start in private medical practice, Sherlock Holmes still came to me from time to time, when he desired a companion in his investigations. But these occasions grew more and more seldom, until I find that in the year 1890 there were only three cases of which I retain any record. During the winter of that year and the early spring of 1891 I saw in the papers that he had been engaged by the French Government upon a matter of supreme importance, from which I gathered that his stay in France was likely to be a long one. It was with some surprise, therefore, that I saw him walk into my consulting-room upon the evening of that 24th of April.

SCENE ONE

[WATSON'S *consulting-room as* HOLMES *enters*]

HOLMES [*wearily*] : Good evening, my dear Watson.

WATSON : Holmes! Bless my soul, I'm delighted to see you. But you're so pale. You've lost weight!

HOLMES : Have you any objection to my closing your shutters?

WATSON [*surprised*] : You're afraid of something?

HOLMES : I am.

WATSON : Of what?

HOLMES : Of air-guns.

WATSON : *Air*-guns?

HOLMES : I think you know well enough, Watson, that I am by no means a nervous man. At the same time, it is stupidity rather than courage not to recognise danger when it's close to you.

WATSON : I say—your knuckles! They're bleeding!

HOLMES : That reminds me, I must beg you to be so unconventional as to let me leave presently by scrambling over your back garden wall.

WATSON : You've been fighting with some villains? They're waiting for you outside?

HOLMES : Just so. Is Mrs Watson in?

WATSON : She is away upon a visit.

HOLMES : Capital!

WATSON : Eh?

HOLMES : It makes it the easier for me to propose that you should come away for a week to the Continent.

WATSON : Where?

HOLMES : Anywhere. It's all the same to me.

WATSON : Er, Holmes, I've been summoned on some pretty odd errands with you in my day, but this is the first time you've suggested anything in the nature of an aimless holiday. If there's something behind all this, then I think you'd better . . .

HOLMES [interrupting him] : You have probably never heard of Professor Moriarty.

WATSON : Moriarty? Never.

HOLMES : There's the genius and the wonder of the thing! This man pervades London, and no one has heard of him. That is what puts him on a pinnacle in the records of crime.

WATSON : He's a criminal, then?

HOLMES : If I could free society of him I should feel that my career had reached its summit. I should be prepared to turn to some more placid line in life. Between ourselves, the recent cases in which I have been of assistance to the Royal Family of Scandinavia and to the French Republic have left me in such a position that I could retire tomorrow. I could live in the quiet fashion which is most congenial to me and concentrate my attention on my chemical researches. But I couldn't rest, Watson, I couldn't sit quiet in my chair if I thought of such a man as Moriarty walking the streets of London unchallenged.

WATSON : What has he done?

HOLMES : He is the Napoleon of crime! He is the organiser of half that is evil and nearly all that is undetected in this city. He's a genius, a philosopher, with a brain of the first order. He sits motionless, like a spider in the centre of its web, but that web has a thousand radiations and he knows well every quiver of each. As you're aware, Watson, no one knows the higher criminal world of London so well as I.

WATSON : Oh, quite, quite.

HOLMES : For years past I have been conscious of some deep organising power standing in the way of the law and throwing its shield over the wrongdoer. In cases of the most varying sorts—forgeries, robberies, murder—I've felt the presence of this force. For years I've tried to break through the veil which shrouded it. And at last the time came when I seized my thread and followed it. And it led me, by way of a thousand cunning windings, to Professor Moriarty, of mathematical celebrity.

WATSON : Great heavens! What has mathematics to do with crime?

HOLMES : A supreme capacity for logical reasoning. Oh, he does little of the actual dirty work himself. He only plans. Is there a paper to be abstracted, we'll say, a house to be rifled, a man to be removed—then word is passed to the Professor, the matter is organised and carried out. The agent may be caught. In that case, money is mysteriously forthcoming for his defence. But the central power which uses the agent is never so much as suspected.

WATSON : Remarkable! What sort of man is he, Holmes?

HOLMES : Good birth, excellent education and endowed by Nature with a phenomenal mathematical faculty. At the age of 21 he wrote a treatise on the binomial theorem which has been acclaimed all over Europe. On the strength of it he won the mathematical chair at one of our smaller universities. To all appearances, he had a brilliant career before him.

WATSON : 'Had'? What went wrong?

HOLMES : Nature's other gift to him was a criminal strain of the most diabolical kind. Instead of his extraordinary mental powers overcoming this they increased it, made it infinitely more dangerous.

WATSON : Well, medical science would agree that that can happen.

HOLMES : *Thank* you, *Doctor*. At any rate, dark rumours gathered round Moriarty in this university town, and he was compelled to resign his chair. He came to London and set up as an army coach.

WATSON : But you say you've penetrated all his secrets now, Holmes. Surely that's the end of him?

HOLMES : Precisely! In three days' time, the Professor and all the principal members of his gang will be in the hands of the police. Then will come the greatest criminal trial of the century.

WATSON : In three days, you say? And yet you're here to suggest we go off to Europe.

HOLMES [*seriously*] : My nerves are fairly proof, Watson. . .

WATSON : None better!

HOLMES : . . . but I must confess to a start when, this morning, I saw the very man who had been so much in my thoughts standing there on the threshold of my room. He is extremely tall and thin. His forehead domes out in a white curve, and his eyes are deeply sunken in his head. He is clean-shaven, pale, retaining something of the professor in his features. His shoulders are rounded from much study, and his face protrudes forward. It is for ever oscillating slowly from side to side in a curiously reptilian fashion.

SCENE TWO

[*A 'flashback' to the parlour of 221B Baker Street*]

MORIARTY : Hm! Hm! Dear me, Mr Holmes, it is a dangerous habit to finger firearms in the pocket of one's dressing-gown.

HOLMES : Pray take a chair, Professor Moriarty. I can spare you five minutes, if you have anything to say.

MORIARTY : All that I have to say has already crossed your mind.

HOLMES : Then possibly my answer has crossed yours.

MORIARTY : You stand fast?

HOLMES : Absolutely. [*Suddenly*] No! Keep your hand from your pocket.

MORIARTY [*sighs*] : I only wish to get out my memorandum

book. There are some dates . . . Ah, yes. I see that you crossed my path on January the fourth. On the 23rd you incommoded me. By the middle of February I was seriously inconvenienced by you. [*Becoming very pained*] At the end of March I was absolutely hampered in my plans. And now at the end of April I find myself placed in such a position through your continual persecution that I am in positive danger of losing my liberty. The situation is becoming an impossible one.

HOLMES : Have you any suggestion to make?

MORIARTY : You must drop it, Mr Holmes. You really must.

HOLMES : Very well. After Monday.

MORIARTY : Tut, tut! I am sure that a man of your intelligence will see that there can be but one outcome to this affair. It has been an intellectual treat to me to see the way you have grappled with it, and it would be a grief to me to be forced to take any extreme measure. You smile, sir, but I assure you that it really would.

HOLMES : Danger is part of my trade.

MORIARTY : This is not danger. It is inevitable destruction. You stand in the way, not merely of an individual, but of a mighty organisation, the full extent of which even you, with all your cleverness, have been unable to realise. You must stand clear, Mr Holmes, or be trodden under foot.

HOLMES : I am afraid that in the pleasure of this conversation I am neglecting business of importance which awaits me elsewhere.

MORIARTY [*sighs again*] : Well, well . . . It seems a pity, but I have done what I could. [*Hard*] I know every move of your game. You hope to place me in the dock. I tell you that I will never stand in the dock. You hope to beat me. I tell you that you will never beat me. If you are clever enough to bring destruction upon me, rest assured that I shall do as much to you.

HOLMES : You have paid me several compliments, Professor Moriarty. Let me pay you one in return when I say that if I were assured of the former eventuality I would, in the interests of the public, cheerfully accept the latter.

MORIARTY [*gravely*] : I can promise you the one—but not the other. Good day to you, Mr Sherlock Holmes.

SCENE THREE

[*In* WATSON'S *consulting-room again*]

HOLMES : That was my singular interview with Professor Moriarty. I confess it left an unpleasant effect on my mind. Even his soft, precise fashion of speech leaves a conviction of sincerity which a mere bully could not produce.

WATSON : But you say you're on the verge of putting him out of harm's way.

HOLMES : My dear Watson, Professor Moriarty is not a man who lets grass grow under his feet. I went out about midday to transact some business in Oxford Street. As I was crossing Welbeck Street a two-horse van, furiously driven, whizzed round and was on me like a flash.

WATSON : By Jove!

HOLMES : I sprang for the footpath and saved myself by the fraction of a second. I kept to the pavement after that, I can tell you, but as I walked down Vere Street a brick came down from the roof of one of the houses. It shattered to fragments at my feet.

WATSON : Holmes, this is dreadful!

HOLMES : Now I have come round to see you, and on my way was attacked by a rough with a bludgeon. I knocked him down, and the police have him in custody. But I can tell you that no possible connection will ever be traced between the gentleman upon whose front teeth I bared my knuckles and the retiring mathematical coach, who is, I dare say, working out problems on a blackboard ten miles away.

WATSON : Well, now I know why you wanted to close the shutters and leave by the back door. But look here, Holmes, why not spend the night here?

HOLMES : No, no, my friend. I have my plans laid and all will be well. Matters have gone so far now that they can move without my help as far as the arrest goes, though my presence will be necessary later for a conviction. I really cannot do better than get away for the next few days until the police can act. So it would be a great pleasure to me if you could accept my invitation to come to the Continent.

WATSON : Well, the practice is quiet. And I have an accommodating colleague.

HOLMES : Capital! We start tomorrow morning, then. These are your instructions, and I beg you to obey them to the letter. You are now playing a double-handed game with me against the cleverest rogue and the most powerful syndicate of criminals in Europe. [*Seriously*] So listen carefully. You will despatch whatever luggage you intend to take by a trusty messenger, unaddressed, to Victoria tonight. In the morning you will send for a hansom, instructing your man to take neither the first nor the second which may present itself.

WATSON : I follow.

HOLMES : You will jump into this hansom and drive to Victoria in time for the Continental express.

WATSON : Where shall I meet you?

HOLMES : At the station. The second first-class compartment from the front will be reserved for you.

WATSON : That carriage is our rendezvous, then?

HOLMES : Yes. And now, my dear Watson, I will take the liberty of finding my way out of your back door and across your garden. Until tomorrow then.

WATSON [*narrating*]: In the morning I obeyed Holmes's injunction to the letter. My luggage was waiting for me at Victoria Station and I had no difficulty in finding the reserved compartment. My only source of anxiety was the non-appearance of Holmes. The station clock marked only seven minutes from the time we were due to start. In vain I searched among the groups of travellers and leave-takers. There was no sign of him. I spent a few minutes in assisting a venerable Italian priest, who was endeavouring to make a porter understand that his luggage was to be booked through to Paris. Then, having taken another look round, I returned to my carriage, where I found that the porter, in spite of the 'Engaged' ticket, had given me my decrepit Italian friend as a travelling companion.

SCENE FOUR

[*In the railway carriage*]

WATSON : Er, signor . . . this is reserved.

HOLMES [*as Italian*] : Signore?

WATSON [*louder*] : Reserved. Engaged.

HOLMES : Ah, engage! [*As if delighted*] Si, si! Engage.

WATSON [*under his breath*] : Oh, lor! [*Normal voice*] My friend . . . and I . . .

HOLMES : Friend!

[*A whistle blows for train to leave*]

Amici! We . . . are . . . friend. Grazie, signore. Grazie!

WATSON [*groans*] : What can have become of him?

HOLMES [*his own voice*]: My dear Watson, you haven't even condescended to say good morning.

WATSON : Great heavens! Holmes! It's you all the time!

HOLMES : Every precaution is still necessary. I have reason to believe . . . Ah!

WATSON : What is it?

HOLMES : See, running along the platform? Moriarty himself!

WATSON : Waving his hands! Trying to get them to stop the train.

HOLMES [*chuckles*] : Too late for that, I fancy.

WATSON : Yes. And we're going too fast for him to jump aboard. He's stopped running. He's just standing there, looking after us.

HOLMES : Capital! But you see, with all our precautions we've cut it rather fine. At least I can now get out of this clerical guise. Have you seen the morning paper, Watson?

WATSON : No, not yet.

HOLMES : You haven't heard about Baker Street, then?

WATSON : Baker Street? Whatever . . .?

HOLMES : They set fire to our rooms last night.

WATSON : Our old rooms!

HOLMES : No great harm was done. They must have lost my track completely after their bludgeon-man was arrested. They must have imagined I had returned there. They have evidently taken the precaution of watching you, though. That is what brought Moriarty to Victoria.

WATSON : Surely, we've shaken him off? This is an express train.

HOLMES : My dear Watson, you evidently don't realise that this man may be taken as being quite on the same intellectual plane as myself. You don't imagine that if I were the pursuer I should allow myself to be baffled by so slight an obstacle?

WATSON : What can he do?

HOLMES : What I should do.

WATSON : But *what?*

HOLMES : Engage a special.

WATSON : You can't engage a special train at half-a-minute's notice.

HOLMES : Anything is possible when one is determined enough. Our train stops at Canterbury for a while, and there is always at least a quarter of an hour's delay at the boat. He will catch us there.

WATSON [*indignantly*] : One would think we were the criminals. Let's have him arrested the moment he arrives.

HOLMES : That would ruin the work of three months. We should get the big fish, but the smaller would dart right and left out of my net. On Monday we should have them all.

WATSON [*sighs*] : What, then?

HOLMES : We shall get out at Canterbury. We must make a cross-country journey to Newhaven, and so over to Dieppe. Moriarty will go on to Paris, trace our luggage there, and wait two days for us at the depot. In the meantime, we shall treat ourselves to a couple of carpet bags, encourage the manufacturers of the countries through which we travel, and make our way at leisure, via Luxembourg, into Switzerland.

WATSON [*narrating*] : We duly alighted at Canterbury, only to find that we should have to wait an hour before we could get a train to Newhaven. I was still looking rather rue-fully after the rapidly-disappearing luggage van which contained my wardrobe, when Holmes pulled my sleeve urgently and pointed up the line. Far away, from among the Kentish woods, there rose a thin spray of smoke. A minute later a carriage and engine could be seen flying along the open curve which leads to the station. We had hardly time to take our place behind a pile of luggage when it passed with a rattle and a roar, beating a blast of hot air into our faces. 'There he goes,' said Holmes, as we watched the carriage swing and rock over the points. 'There are limits to our friend's intelligence, after all. Our only question now is whether to take a premature lunch here, or run our chance of starving before we reach the buffet at Newhaven.'

We made our way to Brussels that night and spent two days there, moving on the third day as far as Strasburg. On Monday morning Holmes had telegraphed to the London police, and in the evening we found a reply waiting for us at our hotel. Holmes tore it open, and then with a bitter curse hurled it into the grate.

SCENE FIVE

[*In* HOLMES' *and* WATSON'S *hotel apartment*]

HOLMES : I might have known it! They have rounded up the whole gang with the exception of him. I think you had better return to England, Watson.

WATSON : Return to England! Whatever for?

HOLMES : Because you will find me a dangerous companion now. This man's occupation is gone. He is lost if he returns to London. If I read his character right he will devote his whole energies to revenging himself upon me. I should certainly recommend you to return to your practice.

WATSON : I shall most certainly do nothing of the kind, Holmes.

HOLMES : My dear Watson, you must realise . . .

WATSON : Not another word, Holmes. I stand by you. We shall leave for Geneva this evening, as arranged.

WATSON [*narrating*] : And for a charming week we wandered up the Valley of the Rhone, and then, branching off at Leuk, we made our way over the Gemmi Pass, still deep in snow, and so, by way of Interlaken, to Meiringen. It was a lovely trip, the dainty green of the spring below, the virgin white of the winter above; but it was clear to me that never for one instant did Holmes forget the shadow which lay across him. In the homely Alpine villages, or in the lonely mountain passes, I could tell, by his quick glancing eyes and his sharp scrutiny of every face that passed us, that he was well convinced that, walk where we would, we could not walk ourselves clear of the danger which was dogging our footsteps. Once, I remember, a large rock which had been dislodged from a ridge clattered down and roared into the lake behind us. In an instant, Holmes had raced up on to the ridge, and was craning his neck in every direction. It was in vain that our guide assured him that a fall of stones was a common chance in the springtime at that spot. He said nothing, but smiled at me with the air of a man who sees the fulfilment of that which he had expected.

HOLMES : I think that I may go so far as to say, Watson, that I have not lived wholly in vain. If my record were closed tonight I could still survey it with equanimity. The air of London is the sweeter for my presence. In over a thousand cases I am not aware that I have ever used my powers upon the wrong side. Of late I have been tempted to look into the problems furnished by Nature, rather than those more superficial ones for which our artificial state of Society is responsible. Your memoirs will draw to an end, Watson, upon the day that I crown my career by the capture or extinction of the most dangerous and capable criminal in Europe.

WATSON [*narrating, gravely*] : I shall be brief, and yet exact, in the little which remains for me to tell. It is not a subject on which I would willingly dwell.

It was on the third of May that we reached the little village of Meiringen, where we put up at the Englischer Hof, then kept by Peter Steiler the elder, an intelligent man who had served for three years as a waiter at the Grosvenor Hotel in London. At his advice we set off next afternoon with the intention of crossing the hills and spending the night at the hamlet of Rosenlaui. We had strict instructions, however, on no account to pass the falls of Reichenbach without making a small detour to see them.

It is, indeed, a fearful place. The torrent, swollen by melting snow, plunges into a tremendous abyss, from which the spray rolls up like smoke from a burning house. The shaft into which the river hurls itself is an immense chasm, lined by glistening, coal-black rock, and narrowing into a creaming, boiling pit of incalculable depth. The long sweep of green water roaring for ever down, and the thick flickering curtain of spray hissing for ever upwards, turn a man giddy with their constant whirl and clamour. We stood near the edge, peering down at the gleam of the breaking water far below us against the black rocks, and listening to the half-human shout which came booming up with the spray out of the abyss.

The narrow path has been cut half-way round the fall to afford a complete view, but it ends abruptly, and the traveller has to return as he came. We had turned to do so when a Swiss lad came running along this path, calling urgently.

SCENE SIX

[*The path above the Reichenbach Falls*]

YOUTH : Herr Doktor, Herr Doktor!

WATSON : What's this, Holmes? Who is he?

HOLMES : I don't recognise him. He seems to know you though.

YOUTH [*panting*]: Herr Doktor! I have . . . I have all the way run.

WATSON : Take your time, my boy. Get your breath first.

YOUTH : No, Herr Doktor, there is no time. The English-woman . . . she will die . . .

WATSON : Englishwoman? What Englishwoman?

YOUTH : At the Hotel . . . The Englischer Hof.

WATSON : We've seen no Englishwoman there—have we Holmes?

YOUTH : She has arrive just after you are leaving. She has collapse and is saying she will die.

HOLMES : Who sent you to us?

YOUTH : Mein Onkle, Herr Steiler.

HOLMES : Why did he not summon the Swiss doctor in the village?

YOUTH : Ja, ja, he has! Aber, the lady is crying, und calling in English that she will some other English see before she will die.

WATSON : Holmes?

HOLMES : Well, you must go, Watson. It is unthinkable to refuse the request of a fellow-countrywoman dying in a strange land.

WATSON : I agree entirely. But won't you come with me? We have managed to stick together from London, and nothing has occurred to you so far. I should not like to think that . . .

HOLMES : No, no, Watson. Your duty is plain. I . . . I think I shall stay here a little while against your return. If I do not see you within the hour, say, I shall walk on slowly over the hill to Rosenlaui, where we will meet again this evening.

WATSON : Very well, Holmes. You will take great care?

HOLMES [*gravely*] : I shall take care.

WATSON : Then, adieu for now.

HOLMES : Adieu . . . for now, my dear Watson.

SCENE SEVEN

[*The hall of the Englischer Hof Hotel*]

WATSON [*puffing*] : Herr . . . Herr Steiler.

STEILER : Herr Dr Watson! You have been running?

WATSON : Where is she?

STEILER : Who?

WATSON : Come along, man, take me to her at once. I'm not too late?

STEILER : Excuse me, Herr Doktor, but I do not understand.

WATSON : The Englishwoman! The one who has been taken ill.

STEILER : There is some mistake. We have no English lady here.

WATSON [*alarmed*] : But . . . the message you sent . . . The boy . . . your nephew . . .

STEILER : I have no nephew, Herr Doktor. I sent no message to you!

WATSON : Great heavens, they've caught up with us after all!

STEILER : Doktor?

WATSON : Has any stranger arrived here since we left?

STEILER : One only—an Englishman. But there was no lady with him.

WATSON : What did he look like?

STEILER : Tall, thin . . . a scholar, I took him to be. But I think you must know him. He asked if you and Herr Holmes were lodging with me.

WATSON : Say no more. Where did he go.

STEILER : I believe he went to take a walk.

WATSON : Herr Steiler, there isn't a moment to lose. I beg you to accompany me to the Reichenbach Falls immediately.

STEILER : Willingly, Doktor. But may I ask . . .?

WATSON : I will explain as we go. But we must not delay one further second. We must hope that we may yet be in time.

SCENE EIGHT

[*Back at the Reichenbach Falls*]

WATSON : There's no sign of him. Pray heaven that he's gone on safely to Rosenlaui.

STEILER : Herr Doktor . . . I have found this.

WATSON : Holmes's alpenstock! Perhaps . . . perhaps he forgot it.

STEILER : There is something else here.

WATSON : What? What is it?

STEILER : These footmarks in the wet ground. Two men.

WATSON : Yes! I see them. But . . . great heavens! They go right to the edge of the chasm . . . and cease.

STEILER : There has been fighting here. See how the ground is all disturbed, and these plants crushed and broken.

WATSON [*stricken*] : No . . . no! It can't be. It can't.

STEILER : There . . . there is no alternative. At the one side, a sheer rock wall. At the other, the chasm.

WATSON : No, no. It's impossible. [*Shouting*] Holmes! Holmes! Holmes!

STEILER [*gently*] : You must keep away from the edge, Doktor. You . . . you can do no good.

WATSON [*controlling himself*] : Thank . . .thank you, Steiler. I . . . I fear you are right. He is gone.

STEILER [*excited*] : See! But here is something!

WATSON [*hopeful*] : What is it? Let me see.

STEILER : A cigarette case, placed on this boulder.

WATSON : It's his. Give me it, please. There's a paper. [*Overjoyed*] Haha! He's gone on to Rosenlaui after all. He's left this message for me to find. You'll see, Herr Steiler. Let me read . . . [*Begins to read*] My dear Watson . . .'

HOLMES [*his voice takes over*] : '. . . My dear Watson, I write these few lines through the courtesy of Professor Moriarty, who awaits my convenience for the final discussion of those questions which lie between us. He has been giving me a sketch of the methods by which he avoided the English police and kept himself informed of our movements. They certainly confirm the very highest opinion which I had formed of his abilities. I am pleased to think that I shall be able to free society from any further effects of his presence, though I fear that it is at a cost which will give pain to my friends, and especially, my dear Watson, to you. I have already explained to you, however, that my career had in any case reached its crisis, and that no possible conclusion to it could be more congenial to me than this. Indeed, if I may make a full confession to you, I was quite convinced that the message from Meiringen was a hoax, and I allowed you to depart on that errand under the persuasion that some development of this sort would follow. Tell Inspector Patterson that the papers which he needs to convict the gang are in pigeon-hole M., done up in a blue envelope and inscribed "Moriarty". I made every disposition of my property before leaving England, and handed it to my brother Mycroft. Pray give my greetings to Mrs Watson, and believe me to be, my dear fellow, very sincerely yours, Sherlock Holmes.'

WATSON [*narrating gravely*] : A few words may suffice to tell the little that remains. An examination by experts leaves little doubt that a personal contest between the two men ended, as it could hardly fail to end in such a situation, in their reeling over, locked in each other's arms. Any attempt at recovering the bodies was absolutely hopeless, and there, deep down in that dreadful cauldron of swirling water and seething foam, will lie for all time the most dangerous criminal and the foremost champion of the law of their generation. The Swiss youth was never found again, and there can be no doubt that he was one of the numerous agents whom Moriarty kept in his employ. As to the gang, it will be within the memory of the public how completely the evidence which Holmes had accumulated exposed their organisation, and how heavily the hand of the dead man weighed upon them. Of their terrible chief few details came out during the proceedings, and if I have now been compelled to make a clear statement of his career it is due to those injudicious champions who have endeavoured to clear his memory by attacks upon . . . [*near to breaking down*] . . . upon him whom I shall ever regard as the best and the wisest man I have ever known.

THE HOUND OF THE BASKERVILLES

Characters in order of appearance:

DR MORTIMER: (elderly)

SHERLOCK HOLMES

DR WATSON

SIR HENRY BASKERVILLE: (Canadian; about thirty)

SOLDIER

BARRYMORE: (middle-aged butler; well-spoken)

BERYL STAPLETON: (mid-thirties; appealing)

STAPLETON: (mid-thirties; dry)

THE HOUND

MRS BARRYMORE: (middle-aged; less 'refined' than her husband)

INSPECTOR LESTRADE: (thirties; risen from the ranks)

THE HOUND OF THE BASKERVILLES

SCENE ONE

[*The parlour of 221B Baker Street.* HOLMES *and* WATSON *rise to greet* DR MORTIMER *and* SIR HENRY BASKERVILLE]

HOLMES : Come in, gentlemen. Dr James Mortimer, I believe?

MORTIMER : The same, sir. Mr Sherlock Holmes, Sir Henry Baskerville.

HOLMES : How do you do? My friend and colleague, Dr Watson.

WATSON : Welcome to 221B Baker Street, Sir Henry.

SIR HENRY : Why, it's a pleasure to set foot on such august premises.

HOLMES : Pray take a seat, gentlemen. Watson has an excellent hand with a decanter.

WATSON : Pleasure, Holmes.

[*He pours drinks for them all*]

HOLMES : You had a pleasant crossing from Canada, Sir Henry?

SIR HENRY : The crossing was fine. I can't say as much for my reception.

HOLMES : By Dr Mortimer?

SIR HENRY [*a laugh*] : Not at all. But for him I shouldn't be troubling you for your advice.

MORTIMER : Mr Holmes, I had no time to explain my urgent request for an appointment. I am a neighbour of Sir Henry's estate in Devonshire, and the family's physician. After the sudden and tragic death of Sir Charles Baskerville, Sir Henry's uncle, I felt it my duty to come to London to greet the new heir and acquaint him with the facts.

HOLMES : Then perhaps you will enlighten us all.

MORTIMER : Mr Holmes, are you familiar with the history of the Baskerville family?

HOLMES : Familiar? No, but I think I recall something. Is there not a legend attached to the Baskerville name? A legend dating from, I think, the seventeenth century. Something about a curse, and a phantom . . .?

MORTIMER : Yes. You are speaking of the Hound of the Baskervilles.

HOLMES : Will you be good enough to refresh my memory, Dr Mortimer? I cannot recall the details of the story.

MORTIMER : Three hundred years ago, Mr Holmes, the lord of the manor of Baskerville was one Sir Hugo, a wild profane, godless man. He expected to have his way with any local girl who took his fancy. One farmer's daughter resisted him, so he and some of his cronies seized her one night and carried her off to the hall. They locked her in a bedchamber to await his attention, while they all enjoyed a few celebratory bottles below. When Sir Hugo eventually went up to claim her he found her gone.

WATSON : She had escaped?

MORTIMER : Yes, by a window. Sir Hugo was like a man possessed. He set the hounds on her, and the evil hunt followed. Sir Hugo galloped ahead of his friends, swearing that he'd find the girl, or give himself to the devil.

WATSON : And . . . did he find her?

MORTIMER : The rest of the hunt finally caught up with the dogs at the rim of a little hollow. They were whimpering and cowering together, hackles erect, hair on end. In the dip lay the poor maid's body, dead of fear and fatigue. And near her . . .

[*He stops*]

WATSON : Yes!

MORTIMER : A sight to freeze the blood. Over the dead body of Sir Hugo Baskerville, plucking at his throat, stood a foul thing—a great black beast shaped like a hound.

WATSON : Great heavens!

MORTIMER : Even as his followers looked the thing tore his throat out. As it turned its blazing eyes and dripping jaws upon them they shrieked with fear and rode screaming away. One died of shock that very night; the others were broken men for the rest of their lives. Such, gentlemen, is the legend of the Hound of the Baskervilles. Since then there have been many sudden and mysterious deaths at Baskerville Hall and the Hound is said to roam the moor by night, seeking further prey.

[*A moment's pause*]

SIR HENRY [*a laugh*] : So that, Mr Holmes, is the four-legged skeleton in my family cupboard.

MORTIMER : You may laugh, if you like, Sir Henry, but there's no one in those parts will set foot on the moor at night, for fear of it.

HOLMES : But I imagine, Dr Mortimer, that you request my help in a matter more recent than the seventeenth century.

MORTIMER : I told you I was the family physician, Mr Holmes. I examined Sir Charles Baskerville after his sudden death. I am not sure if you are aware of its nature?

HOLMES : My friend here is my archivist.

WATSON : I don't recall the precise details.

MORTIMER : Then, allow me to give you them briefly. Sir Charles went out into his grounds one evening, to smoke his after-dinner cigar. When he did not come back his servants went out to search. They found him lying dead.

WATSON : A heart attack?

MORTIMER : Without a doubt. He had suffered from long-standing organic disease. But there were other factors.

HOLMES : Such as?

MORTIMER : I was sent for at once and examined Sir Charles where he lay, on the grass. He was face downward, arms outstretched. His fingers were dug into the ground. His face, when I turned his head, was convulsed with a look of sheer terror.

SIR HENRY : Or maybe the sudden pain . . .

MORTIMER : I glanced around, naturally. It was then that I saw the footprints.

WATSON : Footprints?

HOLMES : A man's, or a woman's?

MORTIMER : Mr Holmes, they were the footprints of a gigantic hound!

[*A pause*]

HOLMES : You saw this?

MORTIMER : As clearly as I see you.

HOLMES : And you said nothing?

MORTIMER : What was the use?

HOLMES : How was it that no one else saw it?

MORTIMER : The marks were some twenty yards from the body, and no one gave them a thought. I don't suppose I should have done if I had not remembered the legend.

HOLMES : If I had only been there! If only you had called me
in sooner, Dr Mortimer.

MORTIMER : I could not, without disclosing these facts to the
world, and I did not wish to start a terrifying rumour.
But now that Sir Henry has received this threat . . .

HOLMES : Threat? What threat?

SIR HENRY : This note, delivered by hand to my hotel.

HOLMES [*reads*] : 'As you value your life or your reason, keep
away from the moor.'

MORTIMER : Dartmoor. Baskerville Hall lies there, close to
Princetown.

WATSON : And Dartmoor Prison.

MORTIMER : That is so.

HOLMES : The message is made up of letters cut from a news-
paper. The Times, if I am not mistaken. But it reads
more as a warning than a threat.

SIR HENRY : That's what I said to Dr Mortimer, but he won't
have it.

MORTIMER : *Why* a warning, if there *is* no threat?

SIR HENRY : I guess it's from some well-meaning local, simple
enough to believe the legend.

HOLMES : But you yourself do not?

SIR HENRY : This is almost the twentieth century. We don't go
in for phantom hounds these days.

WATSON : But the footprints Dr Mortimer found near your
uncle's body?

SIR HENRY : A few blurred marks in wet grass, seen by moon-
light.

HOLMES : All the same, I should like to have seen them. Sir
Henry, may I ask—forgive the unpleasant hypothesis—if you were to go there, and suffered some fatal

accident, who would inherit the Baskerville estate?

SIR HENRY : I'm the last in the direct line. I guess it would go to some cousin.

HOLMES : And the value of the inheritance?

SIR HENRY : I'm told three-quarters of a million sterling.

WATSON : Good heavens!

SIR HENRY : And the property, of course. I guess I'll need that cash to keep the place up—and the Hound in dog biscuits.

MORTIMER : Mr Holmes, won't you try to persuade Sir Henry to take this matter seriously? Convince him that he should not go.

HOLMES : On the contrary. I feel he should go at once.

MORTIMER : But . . .

HOLMES : Only, not alone.

MORTIMER : I shall be travelling down as well.

HOLMES : We must not overlook the possibility that the warning of danger is for some other reason than the legend. Sir Henry must have a companion who can be with him constantly until he is familiar with his surroundings.

SIR HENRY : Come yourself, then. I'd sure like to hear you talk of some of those great cases of yours.

HOLMES : I'm afraid I am too busy, and the criminal classes become restless when I leave London. Besides, the man who is prepared to give you more details of my exploits than I am sits beside you.

SIR HENRY : Dr Watson?

HOLMES : My chronicler, as well as my able assistant.

SIR HENRY : Will you come, Doctor?

WATSON : With the greatest pleasure, Sir Henry.

HOLMES : There is no better man to have at your side if

danger should arise. Now, is there anything more to tell me?

SIR HENRY : Well, since I happen to be here . . .

HOLMES : Yes?

SIR HENRY [*laughs*] : Try this for a mystery. One of my boots was missing from my hotel room after breakfast this morning.

HOLMES : *One* boot?

SIR HENRY : Of a new, unworn pair, what's more. But here's where it gets better. When I went up again after luncheon it was back there in place—but another had gone.

WATSON The other one of the same pair?

SIR HENRY : No. One I'd been wearing when I checked in at the hotel last night.

HOLMES [*lightly*] : Well, no doubt you will find your boot in place when you return. Dr Mortimer, pray escort Sir Henry back. Watson will be there within the hour to accompany you to the train.

MORTIMER : I hope you are regarding this matter seriously, Mr Holmes.

HOLMES : I should not be sparing you the assistance of my valuable associate if I were not. Good day, gentlemen.

SIR HENRY :
MORTIMER : } Good day

[SIR HENRY *and* DR MORTIMER *exit*]

WATSON : Well, Holmes?

HOLMES : Quick, Watson. Give them a moment to leave the premises, then we go after them.

WATSON : What on earth for?

HOLMES : The threat or warning to Sir Henry was delivered by hand to his hotel. Someone has found out where he's staying and may be shadowing him. I wish to know who. Come on!

SCENE TWO

[*A busy London street*]

HOLMES : Keep them in sight and watch for anyone who seems to be doing the same.

WATSON : The pavement's crowded.

HOLMES : There are certain give-away signs . . . Ah!

WATSON : What is it?

HOLMES : That cab. What cab idles along like that with a passenger inside? Note him carefully.

WATSON : A man with a large black beard. You fear he means to attack Sir Henry?

HOLMES : I doubt it . . . Hang it, he's spotted me! The curse of allowing one's features to become familiar in the press.

WATSON : After him, then?

HOLMES : No. If we caught him he would deny any intent. I doubt whether he'll have noted your features, in his shock at seeing me. Keep a sharp lookout for him in future though.

WATSON : Then you *do* regard this business as serious, Holmes?

HOLMES : It is ugly and dangerous, my dear Watson. You must report back to me very carefully. And be sure to keep your old service revolver with you—at all times!

SCENE THREE

[WATSON, SIR HENRY *and* DR MORTIMER *are travel-*
ling across Dartmoor in an open carriage]

WATSON : You must have been very young when you last saw
Baskerville Hall, Sir Henry.

SIR HENRY : I was too small to remember it, Dr Watson. I was
taken to America when my father died. When I got out of
my teens I went to Canada to farm.

MORTIMER : But once a Devon man, always a Devon man.

SIR HENRY : I feel that already, Dr Mortimer. I never saw
scenery to compare with what we've just passed
through. Not quite the same round here, though.

WATSON : Desolate and bleak. More rock than grass.

SIR HENRY : Hello, what's this?

WATSON : A mounted soldier. Rifle at the ready, too! What
does he want?

[*The carriage halts*]

MORTIMER : Yes, my man? What is it?

SOLDIER : Beg pardon, gentlemen. Seen anyone on or near the
road, have you? A man alone, on foot?

SIR HENRY : Not a soul since we left Ashburton, have we?

MORTIMER : A few wagons only. What's this about?

SOLDIER : Escaped convict, sir. Out three days now, but no
sign of him, though every road's being patrolled.

SIR HENRY : All over one man?

SOLDIER : He's no ordinary convict, isn't Selden.

WATSON : Selden! The Notting Hill murderer?

SOLDIER : That's him, sir. Stick at nothing, he wouldn't.

WATSON : No indeed. A ferocious attack on a defenceless girl.

He would certainly have hanged, but for doubts of his sanity.

MORTIMER : Well, I'm afraid we can't help you.

SOLDIER : Very good, sir. Don't any of you gents go wandering on the moor alone till he's safe under lock and key.

SIR HENRY : Thank you for the warning. [*Calling*] Drive on.

> [*The carriage moves on and shortly arrives at Baskerville Hall*]

MORTIMER : Here you are, Sir Henry. You won't mind if I go straight home? My wife's expecting me.

SIR HENRY : Thank you for all you've done, Dr Mortimer.

MORTIMER : I'm sure Barrymore and his wife will look after you as attentively as they did your late uncle.

SIR HENRY : Barrymore?

MORTIMER : Your butler. Coming out of the front door now.

WATSON [*catches his breath*] : A black, bushy beard!

SIR HENRY : How's that, Dr Watson?

WATSON: Oh, er, nothing. Nothing.

MORTIMER: Good evening Barrymore. Here's your new employer.

BARRYMORE : Thank you Dr Mortimer. Welcome to Baskerville Hall, Sir Henry.

SIR HENRY : Well, thank you, Barrymore. This is Dr Watson, who'll be stopping a while.

BARRYMORE : How do you do, sir?

WATSON [*suspiciously*] : We haven't met before, have we?

BARRYMORE : Not that I am aware, sir.

WATSON : Hm!

SIR HENRY : Come on, Watson. If you feel like I do, you'll be ready for a drink and a clean-up—in that order.

SCENE FOUR

[*In Baskerville Hall next morning*]

SIR HENRY : Good morning, Dr Watson.

WATSON : Good morning, Sir Henry.

SIR HENRY : Help yourself to breakfast from the side there. Mrs Barrymore can certainly lay it on.

WATSON : Thank you.

SIR HENRY : Great what a good night's sleep can do. I thought this was a gloomy old barn of a house last night. Did you sleep well?

WATSON : For the most part. Sir Henry, did you hear anything strange, not long after we retired?

SIR HENRY : Why, no, I . . . Wait a minute! There was something.

WATSON : A woman sobbing?

SIR HENRY : That was it. I figured it must be a trick of the wind.

WATSON : I believed so too at first. But . . .

[BARRYMORE *enters*]

SIR HENRY : Ah, Barrymore. Just the man.

BARRYMORE : Sir Henry?

SIR HENRY : Dr Watson and I both fancied we heard a woman sobbing in the house last night. You know anything about that?

BARRYMORE [*a telling hesitation*] : I . . . no, sir.

SIR HENRY : You don't sound too sure.

BARRYMORE [*recovering*] : There are only two women in the house, sir. The scullery-maid sleeps in the other wing, far away from your rooms. The other is Mrs Barrymore. I can assure you it was not my wife you heard.

SIR HENRY : I guess it was the wind then.

BARRYMORE : Most likely, sir.

SIR HENRY : Well, tell Mrs Barrymore I'm delighted to find the old English breakfast still in its glory.

BARRYMORE : Thank you, Sir Henry.

[BARRYMORE *exits*]

SIR HENRY : I've got to start catching up with the paperwork, Watson. What do you plan to do with yourself till luncheon?

WATSON : I thought I might take a stroll upon the moor. Let this good air clear some of the London grime out of my lungs.

SIR HENRY : I wish I could join you. Maybe this afternoon. Watch out for that convict, though.

WATSON : I shall borrow the stoutest stick from the hallstand, if I may.

SIR HENRY : Help yourself. You might even finish up with a reward for catching him.

SCENE FIVE

[WATSON *is tramping alone on Dartmoor, humming as he walks*]

BERYL [*sharply, at his elbow*] : Please . . .!

WATSON [*startled*] : Arrgh!

BERYL : Go back. Back to London. Instantly.

WATSON : Young lady, may I ask what on earth . . .?

BERYL [*low and fast*] : I can't explain. For God's sake, go back and never set foot on the moor again.

WATSON : But I've only just arrived.

BERYL : Can't you tell when a warning is for your own good.
Go away. Leave tonight. Oh! [*Suddenly formal*] Of course,
you're here rather late in the year to see the true beauties
of the place. Now, at the height of summer . . .

[STAPLETON *approaches, carrying a butterfly net*]

STAPLETON : Halloa! Why, Beryl, I lost sight of you.

BERYL : You were so busy chasing that butterfly, I wandered
on.

STAPLETON : A very precious quarry—the Cyclopides is seldom found in late autumn. Well, you have introduced
yourselves, I see.

BERYL : Yes. I was telling Sir Henry it was rather late to see
the moor at its best.

STAPLETON : Sir Henry? [*Laughing*] Oh, dear me!

BERYL : What is it?

WATSON : If you mean Sir Henry Baskerville, madam, I'm
afraid I am not he.

BERYL [*flustered*] : Then . . . we have been talking at cross
purposes.

STAPLETON : You haven't had much time to talk about anything . . . Dr Watson.

WATSON : May I ask how you know my name, Mr . . .?

STAPLETON : Stapleton. Of Merripit House near here. This is
my sister Beryl. I chanced to call on Dr Mortimer this
morning, and he told me you were staying with Sir
Henry. I was certain this stranger on the moor could
only be you. I hope Sir Henry will give Beryl and myself
the pleasure of looking in on us soon? He's well after his
journey?

WATSON : Very well, thank you.

STAPLETON [*slyly*] : And Mr Sherlock Holmes? Ah, you see,

Doctor, your name is as celebrated as your colleague's to those of us who read your accounts of his cases.

WATSON : Mr Holmes, too, is very well, thank you, Mr Stapleton.

STAPLETON : Is he going to honour us with his presence?

WATSON [*cautiously*] : My visit to Sir Henry is a purely personal matter.

STAPLETON : And here was I hoping he was perhaps applying his unique talents to our local tragedy.

WATSON : The death of Sir Charles Baskerville? Surely Dr Mortimer has told you it was from a heart attack?

STAPLETON : Surely he told *you* about the footsteps of the great hound, near the body?

WATSON : He mentioned something of the sort. I happen to be a medical man. We are not too ready to ascribe death to shock from confrontation by spectral hounds.

STAPLETON : Many in these parts would believe it possible. Wouldn't they, my dear?

BERYL : I . . . the legend has a very strong hold.

WATSON : Yet you live in this remote neighbourhood. You evidently wander about freely. And you, sir, your net and box mark you out for a naturalist, ready to roam anywhere the pursuit of a specimen takes you.

STAPLETON : Oh, very good, Doctor! Your esteemed colleague's methods exactly!

WATSON [*pleased*] : Elementary. But aren't you afraid of the Hound?

STAPLETON : My sister and I are not quite so credulous as local folk.

BERYL : Dr Mortimer is not quite 'local folk'.

STAPLETON : No. No, of course you are right, my dear. We all have our little superstitions, though, Doctor, eh?

THE HOUND : [*A distant eerie moaning, 'low and indescribably sad'*]

WATSON : What in heaven's name was that?

THE HOUND : [*We hear it again*]

STAPLETON : It is a timely reminder that there are greater dangers on this moor than any ghostly dog. That is the voice of the great Grimpen Mire—or rather, of some poor pony who has wandered off a path, and set foot in it, to be sucked down to its death.

THE HOUND : [*A final moan*]

WATSON : Horrible!

STAPLETON : A terrible place, the mire. Ah! There goes my Cyclopides again. Get you yet, my beauty!

[STAPLETON *dashes off*]

WATSON : Your brother is a true enthusiast, Miss Stapleton.

BERYL : He . . . he is a little teasing at times. [*Low, urgent*] Dr Watson, I apologise for mistaking you for Sir Henry. But if you have any influence with him, please take him away from here.

WATSON : But why? Not because of the Hound, surely?

BERYL : Yes.

WATSON : You don't mean you believe in it?

BERYL : Dr Mortimer does. Isn't that enough for you?

WATSON : As your brother says . . .

BERYL : Believe *me*. Please.

STAPLETON [*calling*] : Beryl! I have him. Come along, my dear.

BERYL [*calling*] : Coming! [*Low and fierce*] This may be my last chance, Doctor. I warn you, with all my heart, that Sir Henry Baskerville must be got away from this place immediately. If he is not, then he may never leave it alive!

SCENE SIX

[WATSON *and* SIR HENRY *occupy armchairs in Bask-*
erville Hall]

SIR HENRY : . . . So you reckon, Dr Watson, that Miss Stapleton's warning was meant for me?

WATSON : I am positive, Sir Henry. She urged me to persuade
you to go away from these parts at once.

SIR HENRY : All because of the Hound of the Baskervilles?

WATSON : Yes. Only, she had no time to explain.

SIR HENRY : She was afraid her brother might overhear?

WATSON : Yes. He had already scoffed at the legend. Perhaps
she was anxious not to invite further scorn. And yet,
remember it was because of an earlier warning that I am
here to guard you at all. And if the Hound were in some
way connected with your late uncle's death . . .

SIR HENRY [*smiling*] : You know what I reckon, Doctor? Here's
a young girl—pretty, you say . . .

WATSON : Extremely.

SIR HENRY : . . . living alone with her brother in the wilds of
Dartmoor. No place to go, and not much company. I
guess she's looking for a little drama in her life, so she's
let herself get obsessed with this legend. Her brother's
trying to get her out of it, and he's inclined to get mad at
her for speaking about it to strangers. How's that for
amateur psychology?

WATSON : Plausible, except for that other warning in London,
which I am certain cannot have been delivered by her.

SIR HENRY : By all accounts, half the population round here
believe the Hound exists. Tell you what, why don't I
accept that invitation of Stapleton's to drop in on them?

WATSON : I'm not sure how wise . . .

SIR HENRY : Oh, come on! No danger from a guy who spends his time netting butterflies. I'd quite like to get a look at his pretty sister.

WATSON [*chuckling*] : Oh, very well. But Holmes would insist I escort you.

SIR HENRY : Chaperon, you mean? O.K., then. It's a fine day. We'll walk over to Merripit House after lunch.

SCENE SEVEN

[WATSON, SIR HENRY *and the* STAPLETONS *taking tea in Merripit House*]

STAPLETON : You'll take another cup of tea, Sir Henry? Beryl, my dear, Sir Henry's cup.

BERYL [*she is subdued throughout*] : Yes, John. Dr Watson?

WATSON : Well, just one more, Miss Stapleton, thank you.

SIR HENRY : It's been a pleasant meeting, Mr Stapleton. Just as soon as I'm properly settled into the Hall you and your sister must come over and dine.

STAPLETON : Oh, that would be a great pleasure. Wouldn't it, Beryl?

BERYL : Yes. Thank you, Sir Henry.

SIR HENRY : I guess there's not much socialising in these parts.

STAPLETON : Very little, very little. But we're quite content with our own company, aren't we?

BERYL : Oh . . . oh yes. Quite content.

WATSON : May I ask what brought you here? You are a North Countryman, I believe?

STAPLETON : Ah, the great detective's disciple again! I suppose the traces of accent still linger, though. I had a school in the North until an epidemic broke out and three of the boarders died. The parents of the rest took them away, and that was the end of it. Quite a blow at the time wasn't it, Beryl?

BERYL : It was very worrying.

STAPLETON : However, out of misfortune came the freedom to give unlimited time to my botanical and zoological interest. This is a good region for a naturalist, and we were delighted to find this house, weren't we?

BERYL : Yes, John.

SIR HENRY : Do you share your brother's interest, Miss Stapleton?

BERYL : I . . . well, I . . .

STAPLETON : Indeed she does, Sir Henry. Beryl is as devoted to Nature as I am.

[*A slightly embarrassed pause*]

WATSON : Tell me, Mr Stapleton, the hillside there—I have been observing it from your window.

STAPLETON : The tor, it's called.

WATSON : Those stone rings, scattered about its sides. Are they sheep pens?

STAPLETON : They are the homes of our worthy ancestor, prehistoric man. He grazed his cattle on the slopes and dug for tin. The moor was far more populated then.

SIR HENRY : A good place for that escaped convict to hide out, eh? Don't you worry about him, living in so remote a place?

STAPLETON : We keep our door and windows locked, and hope they'll catch him soon.

SIR HENRY [*casually*] : And this so-called Hound of the Baskervilles? It doesn't trouble you at all?

STAPLETON [*firmly*] : Our interest is in natural things, Sir
Henry, not supernatural ones. [*Suddenly unctuous*] Now,
you will have just one more cup of tea before you leave?
Beryl, Sir Henry's cup.

BERYL : Yes, John, dear. [*Risking it*] . . . just one more cup, Sir
Henry. Before you *leave*.

SCENE EIGHT

> [WATSON *and* SIR HENRY *are enjoying a nightcap in
> Baskerville Hall*]

SIR HENRY : One more glass, eh, Watson?

WATSON : A small one, thank you. [*Yawns*] Do excuse me, Sir
Henry.

SIR HENRY : Well, I guess that's all there is to it. With that
legend, and my uncle's sudden death and a rumour of
the Hound's footprints near him, I guess it's gotten into
the girl's mind that something like it's lined up for me,
too.

WATSON : All the same, I should be happier if Holmes were
here. He would know the true answer in an instant.

SIR HENRY : You're keeping him fully informed, aren't you?

WATSON : A daily bulletin. He doesn't reply, though. If and
when he believes it necessary, he'll come here.

SIR HENRY [*stretching*] : Right. I'm going up now.

WATSON : Yes, so am I.

> [*They get to their feet*]

SIR HENRY : We'd better turn off the lamps as we go. I sent Barrymore off duty for the night.

WATSON : I'll do this one . . .

MRS BARRYMORE : [*Distant sobbing*]

WATSON : Sir Henry! Listen!

MRS BARRYMORE : [*More sobbing*]

WATSON [*low*] : It's that sobbing sound again.

SIR HENRY : That's no wind. That's the real thing.

MRS BARRYMORE : [*More sobbing. It ceases abruptly*]

WATSON : It *must* be Mrs Barrymore.

SIR HENRY : It sounded as if a door were open for a few seconds. Now it's closed again. That's why we can't hear it any more.

WATSON [*whispers urgently*] : Sir Henry, put your lamp out, quickly. Can you hear footsteps?

SIR HENRY [*low*] : I guess I can.

WATSON : Mrs Barrymore is in their room, sobbing bitterly. He's come out·and left her there.

SIR HENRY : What's he doing, creeping about at midnight.

WATSON : We can find out. Can you get to the stairs in the dark?

SIR HENRY : I'm almost with you.

WATSON : Then, if we go up quietly . . . watch out, there's a light . . .

SIR HENRY [*whispering*] : Look! At the half-landing window . . . [*Calling sharply*] Barrymore! That you?

BARRYMORE [*slightly off*] : Ah!

> [SIR HENRY *and* WATSON *run up stairs.* BARRYMORE *stands at a window with a lamp in his hand*]

SIR HENRY : What d'you think you're doing, man?

BARRYMORE : I . . . I fancied that I might not have locked this window securely, sir. I came out to see.

SIR HENRY : Leaving your wife sobbing her heart out in your room?

WATSON : Give me that lamp, Barrymore.

SIR HENRY : What is it, Watson?

WATSON : Stand clear of the light and shade your eyes, Sir Henry. Look up towards the tor. See there—a pinprick of light?

[*Slight pause*]

SIR HENRY : By Harry, you're right!

WATSON : Watch it closely as I move the lamp across the window.

[*He passes the lamp to and fro*]

SIR HENRY [*a gasp*] : It's moving, too!

WATSON : Responding to my signal. Eh, Barrymore?

SIR HENRY : What does this mean? I want the truth, man.

MRS BARRYMORE [*suddenly close*] : I'll tell you, Sir Henry.

BARRYMORE : No, Eliza!

MRS BARRYMORE : It's got to come out, John. I can't stand the strain no longer. That light on the tor, sir. It's my brother.

SIR HENRY : Your brother?

MRS BARRYMORE : The escaped convict, Selden. Please don't blame my husband, sir. It was all for me and my poor brother, out there starving on the moor. He managed to get word to me that he's hiding in one of the stone huts. He was desperate for food and warm clothes. Each night we put something out for him at a place on the wall, and Barrymore signals him it's safe to come and fetch it. [*Breaking down*] I don't care what he is, or what he's done. He's my flesh and blood, and I can't let him starve.

WATSON : He would do better to give himself up, Barrymore. Can't you see that?

BARRYMORE : I know that, sir. We both do. But I know him. He never will.

WATSON : Then he risks being shot.

MRS BARRYMORE : It's what frightens me most, sir. I wouldn't care about him being behind bars again. [*Renewed sobbing*]

SIR HENRY : Barrymore, take your wife back to your room.

BARRYMORE : Yes, Sir Henry.

SIR HENRY : I understand what you've done. I'll make sure everything possible's done to take him without harm.

MRS BARRYMORE : God bless you, sir! God bless you!

BARRYMORE : Come on, love.

[*He escorts his wife away, still sobbing*]

SIR HENRY : O.K., Watson. You game?

WATSON : What for?

SIR HENRY : We go up there and take him ourselves.

WATSON : But we'll never find him in the dark.

SIR HENRY : If I could find an injured animal by night on thirteen thousand Canadian acres, I guess I can find a man on an English hillside. I got a bearing on his light by the stars.

WATSON : We might meet him on his way down to pick up his provisions.

SIR HENRY : O.K., then. Hurry and fetch that revolver of yours, and we're on our way!

SCENE NINE

> [SIR HENRY *and* WATSON *are picking their way across the dark moorland*]

WATSON [*low, breathing heavily*] : No sight nor sound. He'll have heard us and gone into hiding.

SIR HENRY : Then we'll do the same. If we stay quiet long enough he'll make some move.

WATSON : If he's away from his hideout he won't want to be seen by dawn light.

THE HOUND : [*Distant cry as earlier*]

SIR HENRY : What in Hades is that?

WATSON : The great Grimpen Mire has another victim, I fear. Some unfortunate pony.

SIR HENRY : A pony? Sounded to me . . . [*He stops*]

WATSON : Yes?

SIR HENRY : It sounded like the baying of a hound.

WATSON : Hush! Look over there!

SIR HENRY : What?

WATSON : There. Just over to the left.

SIR HENRY : It's a light! We must have come further than we reckoned. He's either still in his lair, or he's beaten us back to it.

WATSON : Then we have him. Shall I lead?

SIR HENRY : Got your gun?

WATSON : I have.

> [*He draws his revolver*]

Quickly, but quietly.

> [*They cautiously approach one of the stone huts*]

WATSON [*very low*] : Right. He's inside that hut, and there'll only be the one entrance. Here goes!

[*They rush into the stone hut*]

All right, Selden. Put up your hands, and no harm will come to you!

[*Slight pause*]

HOLMES : My dear Watson!

WATSON : Holmes!

HOLMES : Do come in. Welcome to my humble, though I am pleased to say temporary, abode!

SCENE TEN

[*In the stone hut, as before*]

SIR HENRY : Mr Holmes! What in heaven's name are you doing hiding out in the wilds of Dartmoor? You *are* hiding out, aren't you?

HOLMES : Yes, Sir Henry. Until our intrepid friend Watson came charging in with that revolver. Please apply the safety catch, there's a good fellow.

WATSON : Oh yes.

[*He does so*]

But Holmes, I thought you were still at Baker Street.

HOLMES : That is what I wished you to think.

[*They all sit on the floor*]

WATSON : You didn't trust me to be able to handle this matter on my own?

HOLMES : Nothing of the sort. Your reports, which have been brought to me here by the most secret of hands, have proved invaluable to my investigation.

SIR HENRY : Then why live in a stone hut in the wilds, when you could have had the comfort of Baskerville Hall?

HOLMES : Because had I been there I should have witnessed things from the same viewpoint as yourselves. And whoever is at the heart of this matter would have known of my presence and kept on his guard. But tell me, how did you track me down?

SIR HENRY : There's an escaped convict on the moor. We came to take him.

WATSON : Selden. The Notting Hill murderer, remember?

HOLMES : Ah yes. Then he must be the other man I've seen lurking in this wasteland.

SIR HENRY : He turns out to be the brother of Mrs Barrymore, my butler's wife. They'd been sending him out food and some of my old clothes till we caught Barrymore signalling from one of my windows.

HOLMES : So you decided to take him yourselves? Didn't it occur to you, Watson, that you might be exposing Sir Henry to the very perils I sent you to guard him against?

SIR HENRY : I'm my own keeper, Mr Holmes. It was my idea to take Selden humanely, rather than leave him to be shot down by some searcher. Dr Watson stuck to his duty by accompanying me.

WATSON : And what is more, Holmes, as I indicated in one of my reports, Barrymore has a full black beard.

SIR HENRY : A beard? What's that to do with anything?

HOLMES : I chose not to tell you, Sir Henry, that while you were in London you were being shadowed by a black-bearded man.

SIR HENRY : The guy who handed in that warning that if I came to Dartmoor I'd be risking my life?

HOLMES : I fancy that was someone else. Our bearded friend was more probably one of those the warning was intended *against*.

SIR HENRY : You're making it sound like some kind of gang's after me. I thought the danger was supposed to be the Hound of the Baskervilles—if there is such a thing.

HOLMES : I'm certain there is. I have heard its howling.

WATSON : Ah, Holmes, I can explain that. It's the dying moans of unfortunate moor ponies, drowning in the Grimpen Mire.

HOLMES : Who told you that?

WATSON : The fellow Stapleton I've mentioned in my reports. The naturalist who lives with his sister.

SIR HENRY : He reckons the Hound's nothing but a legend.

HOLMES : Though his sister does not, I gather.

WATSON : She seems convinced it's real. She was most anxious I should persuade Sir Henry to get away from here.

HOLMES : A second warning, eh? Did it occur to you she might have been responsible for the first, in London?

SIR HENRY [*laughs*] : I don't see Miss Beryl Stapleton taking a day trip to London to deliver a warning to a guy she's never met, staying at a hotel she couldn't know he'd be at. That brother of hers hardly lets her out of his sight.

HOLMES : Ah, well. I fancy your convict will have heard us by now, and gone to ground for the night. You had better be getting back to the Hall.

SIR HENRY : Won't you come now, Mr Holmes?

HOLMES : I prefer to keep my presence a secret for a little longer. I have most of the strands of the mystery in my hands already.

SIR HENRY : You *have?*

HOLMES : There remain only one or two further points to be proved. Sir Henry, I should like to have a couple of minutes' private consultation with our friend Watson. There are some particulars it is best for you not to know, if you are to continue to act out your part innocently.

SIR HENRY [*chuckles*] : Setting me up as a decoy, eh?

HOLMES : Something of the sort.

SIR HENRY : Well, I'll set off back by the way we came. Selden won't show himself now.

WATSON : I shall be after you directly, Sir Henry.

SIR HENRY [*exiting*] : Don't worry. I'll be O.K.

WATSON : Well, Holmes?

HOLMES : First of all, the butler Barrymore is not the bearded man we saw in London. I have made discreet enquiries of local tradespeople, and he was seen in *this* neighbourhood by several of them on that day.

WATSON : Then he's ruled out.

HOLMES : *He* was not in London, but the Stapletons were.

WATSON : What!

HOLMES : A simple enquiry at the railway station. You see the value of my being here incognito.

WATSON : It could be coincidence.

HOLMES : Scarcely, when she is the one so anxious to warn Sir Henry of his danger. There is one other detail . . .

WATSON : What is that?

HOLMES : They are not. . .

THE HOUND : [HOLMES *is interrupted by a terrible baying howl, some little way off*]

WATSON : My God!

THE HOUND : [*A further howl, with a snarl in it. A man's screams*]

WATSON : Sir Henry! The Hound has got him!

HOLMES : Quick Watson!

> [*They run out of the hut and over stony ground. We hear the Hound and more screams. Both cease suddenly, leaving only* HOLMES *and* WATSON *running*]

HOLMES : By heaven, if we're too late. . .!

WATSON : Over here, I think.

HOLMES : If you see it, shoot!

WATSON : I've found him. Quick!

> [*They stoop over a man's body*]

HOLMES [*panting heavily*] : Is he dead? . . . I . . . shall . . . never . . . forgive myself . . .

WATSON : He must have fallen from that rock in his flight.

HOLMES : Any pulse?

WATSON : I think . . . No. None.

HOLMES : This is my doing. I should never have asked him to go on alone.

WATSON : You couldn't know the Hound would appear. Was it real, or a spectre? I didn't see it.

HOLMES : Nor I. But whichever it was, it frightened Sir Henry to his death, just as it did his uncle.

WATSON : There's neither sign nor sound of it now.

HOLMES : This is a catastrophe. Better strike a light. See whether he was actually savaged.

> [HOLMES *strikes a match*]

WATSON : I'll turn him over . . . Holmes! This isn't Sir Henry!

HOLMES [*a sigh of relief*] : No this is Selden, the convict. But . . . another match.

> [*He strikes another*]

I thought so. He wasn't wearing this suit when I saw him. He had on his prison clothes.

WATSON : This must be Sir Henry's old suit. The one the Barrymores gave him.

HOLMES : Then my case is complete.

WATSON : How does this settle it?

HOLMES : Don't you see? It was Sir Henry's scent—his clothing—that drew the beast to him.

WATSON : But how could it know?

HOLMES : Remember the strange theft of Sir Henry's boot at his London hotel?

WATSON : You laughed that off as an everyday mischance.

HOLMES : The first boot, yes. It was brand new and never worn by Sir Henry. But whoever took it realised his mistake, replaced it, and removed a worn one. That, coupled with the Hound's footprints close to Sir Charles Baskerville's body, struck me as most significant.

WATSON : Someone took the boot to acquaint the Hound with its intended victim's scent?

HOLMES : Precisely. The Hound was obviously no phantom, and Sir Henry's life was really in danger, as we have just seen.

WATSON : But for the grace of God it would have found him instead of chancing on this poor devil first.

HOLMES : Such are the workings of Fate, Watson. Listen!

WATSON [low] : Someone's coming. Sir Henry returning, maybe?

STAPLETON [nearby] : Holloa! Anybody there?

WATSON : That's Stapleton.

HOLMES : Say nothing about the background to this matter. Leave it to me.

[STAPLETON *approaches*]

STAPLETON : Anybody there? Why, Dr Watson, it's you. I heard cries and . . . who's this? Don't say it's Sir Henry!

WATSON : It is the escaped convict, Selden.

STAPLETON [*shaken*] : But . . . how . . .? [*A second's pause; he swallows and collects himself*] Thank God it wasn't Sir Henry.

HOLMES : Why Sir Henry, might I ask?

STAPLETON : Ah, Mr Sherlock Holmes, I perceive.

HOLMES : You are quick at identification, Mr . . .?

STAPLETON : Stapleton. We've been expecting you in these parts since Dr Watson came down. You're just in time for a tragedy.

HOLMES : But *why* suppose this to be Sir Henry?

STAPLETON : Oh, well, following the tragic death of his uncle, I rather feared . . .

HOLMES : I see. Did you by any chance hear anything besides the cries which brought you here?

STAPLETON : Nothing at all.

HOLMES : We fancied there was an animal-like howling.

STAPLETON [*easier now*] : Oh, not that Hound again! I've explained that sound to Dr Watson. It's made by ponies sinking into the Grimpen Mire.

HOLMES : You should have told me, Watson.

WATSON : Eh? But . . .

HOLMES : Then the recollection I shall carry back with me to London tomorrow will be one of a straightforward mishap, without any significance.

STAPLETON : You're going back so soon?

HOLMES : Yes, and taking my friend here with me.

STAPLETON : I'm sorry. My sister Beryl and I would have liked you both to come with Sir Henry to dine with us tomorrow. We have little company, especially of such distinction.

HOLMES : A kindly thought, but I must not linger. I'm sure Sir Henry will accept your invitation for himself though, won't he Watson?

WATSON [*bewildered*] : Oh, I, er, I'm sure . . .

HOLMES : We'll convey it to him, if you wish.

STAPLETON : I am most grateful. Eight o'clock say? But what about this poor fellow?

HOLMES : We'll deal with him.

STAPLETON : Then I'd better be getting back. My sister worries a little over my nocturnal strolls. Goodnight gentlemen. Perhaps another time.

[STAPLETON *goes*]

WATSON : Goodnight.

HOLMES : So that's our former schoolmaster in the North of England, who had to close his school because of scandal.

WATSON : I understood it was due to an epidemic.

HOLMES : I imagine that is the reason he gives. But there are scholastic agencies through which it's possible to trace any man who has been in the profession. I know all about him.

WATSON : Was his sister involved, too?

HOLMES : Not at all.

WATSON : I must say I wouldn't have thought it of her. Timid, but quite charming.

HOLMES : My dear Watson, I know your susceptibilities. In case she has aroused your interest, I must warn you that she's already married.

WATSON : She is? To whom?

HOLMES : To Stapleton.

WATSON : His wife! Then why on earth this masquerade?

HOLMES : I expect to be able to explain it soon enough. But let's cover up this fellow. He'll be all right here till morning. Now that my presence is known, I'll come with you to Baskerville Hall and beg Sir Henry's hospitality for the night.

WATSON : Holmes, is it really wise for us both to go back to London tomorrow?

HOLMES : I will explain to Sir Henry why it is for the best. By the bye, one small caution.

WATSON : Yes?

HOLMES : Say nothing to him about his narrow escape tonight. It would be a pity to spoil his appetite for dining with the Stapletons. I fancy it is going to prove an engagement he will never forget—for as long as he lives!

SCENE ELEVEN

> [*In Baskerville Hall.* SIR HENRY, WATSON *and* BARRYMORE *are comforting* MRS BARRYMORE. HOLMES *is examining the family portraits*]

MRS BARRYMORE : [*Sobbing*]

SIR HENRY : I'm truly sorry about your brother, Mrs Barrymore. He must have stumbled off a rock while roaming the moor in the dark.

WATSON : He died instantly.

BARRYMORE : That's right, love. He'd have gone on suffering

while he stayed on the run, and he'd have been shot down sooner or later . . .

MRS BARRYMORE : My own flesh and blood!

BARRYMORE : . . . or gone back to jail, to rot his life away.

SIR HENRY : You'd better take your wife upstairs, Barrymore. Make her take that draught Dr Watson's given you. I'll arrange for Selden's body to be collected in the morning.

BARRYMORE : Thank you, Sir Henry—gentlemen. Come on, love.

[*He helps her away. Sobs recede*]

WATSON : A sad business for them. I suppose he was the rotten apple in the barrel.

HOLMES [*nearby*] : Sir Henry!

SIR HENRY : Yes, Mr Holmes?

HOLMES : This is an extremely fine series of portraits you have here. Family, I presume?

SIR HENRY : Why, yes. Barrymore's been telling me who they all are.

HOLMES : Watson won't allow that I know anything of art, but that one's a Kneller, I'll swear, and this one a Reynolds.

SIR HENRY : The guy with the telescope? I'm told he's Rear Admiral Baskerville. Served under Rodney in the West Indies.

HOLMES : And this cavalier?

SIR HENRY [*laughs*] : Talking of rotten apples, he's the wicked Sir Hugo in person. You'll excuse me, gentlemen, I must go and see that the Barrymores are O.K. I feel responsible for them. I'll see you shortly for brandy and a cigar.

[*Sir Henry exits*]

HOLMES : So this is the swashbuckling Hugo. The start of the legend of the Hound.

WATSON : And its first victim.

HOLMES : Does he remind you of anyone?

WATSON : Eh? Not Sir Henry.

HOLMES : If I mask the hat and ringlets with my arm.

> [*He covers part of the portrait, leaving the face revealed*]

WATSON : Great . . . great heavens! Stapleton, to the life!

HOLMES : A most interesting instance of a throwback. The fellow is a Baskerville descendant for certain. Now my case really is complete.

WATSON : I have it! He's after the inheritance.

HOLMES : Most certainly. But by this time tomorrow he'll be fluttering in our net as helpless as one of his own butterflies. We'll add him to the Baker Street collection.

WATSON : If you're so sure of him, why not have him arrested at once?

HOLMES : Proof my dear Watson. I'm morally certain now that the man moved into these parts with his plan already made. There were only two descendants between him and the inheritance. Sir Charles, he knew, had a weak heart. He managed to scare him to death. Sir Henry, whom he took the precaution of observing in London, promised to be a tougher proposition. The Hound would need to do more than growl at him.

WATSON : You mean to say Stapleton is the Hound's keeper—it's owner?

HOLMES : Precisely. The legend of a spectral beast suited him perfectly. He obtained a real one and used it to dispose of Sir Charles. It would have done for Sir Henry this evening if the escaped convict hadn't chanced to get in its way, wearing his cast-off clothes.

WATSON : Then all we have to do is prove that he possesses such a beast.

HOLMES : But where were the marks of its fangs on Sir Charles? Or Selden?

WATSON : Both died before the Hound reached them. A hound would not bite a corpse.

HOLMES : Therefore, how do we prove that a hound was in the plot at all? Without that, and without linking the beast to Stapleton, we have no case. That is why the situation justifies our running any risk in order to complete one.

WATSON : You mean . . . Sir Henry . . .!

HOLMES : That is the reason I asked you to say nothing to him of the Hound's involvement in tonight's death. When he goes to dine with the Stapletons tomorrow he must do so unsuspectingly.

WATSON : You want him to go there as innocent bait . . .

HOLMES : Exactly.

WATSON : Whilst we make our peaceful way back to London . . .! Holmes, that is intolerable! You are prepared to sacrifice a life in order to support a theory.

HOLMES : Expediency must occasionally over-rule principle. Now here comes Sir Henry. Not a word to him, mind, or he might cancel his dinner engagement, and that would not suit my book at all.

WATSON : Oh, very well, Holmes.

SCENE TWELVE

[*Outside the railway station.* SIR HENRY *is taking leave of* HOLMES *and* WATSON]

SIR HENRY : Well, I'm sorry to see you leaving, Mr Holmes. And you, Dr Watson.

HOLMES : Our remaining would seem superfluous, Sir Henry. There has been no sign of any hound—no attempt upon your life. I am convinced those warnings you received were from gullible folk who take the legend of the Hound of the Baskervilles seriously.

SIR HENRY : I guess you're right. Now that the escaped convict's out of the way I dare say things will settle down.

HOLMES : I am sure of it. I hope you will enjoy a pleasant evening with the Stapletons. Please give them our renewed regrets, and say we really had to get back to London.

SIR HENRY : I will. Well, goodbye, gentlemen. Sorry to have dragged you down here on a fool's errand.

HOLMES : Not at all.

WATSON : Goodbye Sir Henry.

SIR HENRY : Hup there!

[*His vehicle rattles off*]

WATSON : Holmes, I don't like . . .

[*Whistle of approaching train*]

HOLMES : Nicely timed. Here comes our train.

WATSON : No, Holmes. The Up platform is the other side. This is the train *from* London.

HOLMES : Nevertheless, it is the one which interests us. Come along.

[*He leads the way across the bridge to the opposite platform as the train pulls in.* INSPECTOR LESTRADE *alights from the train, sees them and approaches*]

LESTRADE : Mr Holmes! Dr Watson!

WATSON : Inspector Lestrade!

HOLMES : Good afternoon, Lestrade. I thought for a moment you weren't on the train.

LESTRADE : Only just caught it.

HOLMES : You've brought a warrant?

LESTRADE : I went to apply for it the moment I got your telegram this morning. I was kept waiting so long I almost missed the train.

HOLMES : Capital! You're armed, I hope?

LESTRADE : As long as I have my trousers, I've a hip pocket. And as long as I've a hip pocket, I've something in it.

HOLMES : Watson, you had better retrieve your own revolver from your valise.

WATSON : Holmes, I really do wish you'd tell me what your game is.

HOLMES : *Our* game, my dear Watson, is a waiting one. We must all stay out of everyone's sight until dusk, when we shall make our stealthy way to the Stapletons' house, and watch for the outcome of their dinner party. It promises to be a lively one.

SCENE THIRTEEN

> [*Night.* HOLMES, WATSON *and* LESTRADE *are concealed behind shrubbery in view of Merripit House*]

HOLMES [*low*] : Watson, you've been inside this house before.

WATSON : Yes.

HOLMES : You're sure that door is the one Sir Henry will come out by?

WATSON : Positive. There is only the Grimpen Mire behind the cottage.

HOLMES : Then we stay in our position here, with an excellent line of view through the window.

LESTRADE : So long as the fog holds off. I can see them still at table. The two men, at any rate. No sign of the woman.

WATSON : Perhaps she is in the kitchen. The Stapletons keep no servant.

WATSON : The fog's moving towards us, Holmes.

HOLMES : The one thing on earth which could disarrange my plans! It's already ten o'clock. Sir Henry's life may depend on his coming out before the fog is over the path.

LESTRADE : We may soon have to move onto higher ground! If he isn't out in quarter of an hour we won't be able to see our hands in front of us.

HOLMES : We dare not move any further. We cannot take the chance that Sir Henry will be overtaken before he reaches us!

WATSON : Overtaken by . . . the Hound?

HOLMES : I fear so . . . yes.

LESTRADE : They've got up from the table. He's helping him on with his coat.

HOLMES : Thank heaven!

LESTRADE : Still no sign of her, though.

WATSON : The door. Sir Henry's coming out.

HOLMES : Stapleton has gone back inside. It's as I thought. Get your pistols ready.

[ALL *cock their revolvers*]

WATSON : Here comes Sir Henry.

HOLMES : Yes—and the Hound after him.

[*Baying of Hound distant, then louder as it passes. A cry of terror from Sir Henry*]

HOLMES [*shouting*] : Now! Quickly, for God's sake—quickly!

[*Each fires at the Hound as it chases* SIR HENRY *past. The Hound's cry changes to a ghastly, wounded shriek, then silence*]

WATSON : Quick! Sir Henry!

[*They run to where he lies beside the Hound*]

Sir Henry!

SIR HENRY [*gasping*] : I'm . . . I'm . . . O.K. Just . . . winded . . .

LESTRADE : I thought we'd missed—the way that creature still went on!

HOLMES : Sheer weight and momentum carried it.

WATSON : Look, Holmes. This ghastly green effect about its jowls. Phosphorescent paint.

[*They help* SIR HENRY *to his feet*]

HOLMES : Now for the fiend responsible.

LESTRADE : He'll have heard the shots. He'll know the game's up!

HOLMES : Come on, then!

[HOLMES, WATSON *and* LESTRADE *run to Merripit House.* LESTRADE *shoulders the door open and they run inside*]

LESTRADE : Come out, Stapleton, in the name of the law!

BERYL : [*Muffled cries. She is gagged*]

WATSON : Mrs Stapleton!

HOLMES : Quick, untie her! Mrs Stapleton . . .

BERYL : [*Gasping as she is freed*]

HOLMES : You must tell us where your husband is.

BERYL : Is he safe?

LESTRADE : He won't escape us, madam.

BERYL : I didn't mean my husband. Is Sir Henry safe?

WATSON : Quite safe. The Hound is dead.

BERYL : Thank God! Thank God!

LESTRADE : Your husband?

HOLMES : There is only one way he can have gone—across the Grimpen Mire.

WATSON : He'll never find his way in this fog.

BERYL [*passionately*] : Then let him drown!

STAPLETON : [*A distant cry as he sinks into the mire*]

BERYL : The villain! He dragged *me* down into the mire when he made me his dupe and his slave. I was supposed to be the bait to lure Sir Charles and his nephew to their deaths. I tried to warn Sir Henry. . .

HOLMES : In London too?

BERYL : Yes. When that villain was following him.

HOLMES : In disguise? A black beard?

BERYL : Yes.

[SIR HENRY *enters*]

SIR HENRY : I heard a man's cries.

WATSON : Your would-be murderer, Stapleton. He's drowned in the Grimpen Mire.

SIR HENRY : Good Lord!

HOLMES : He made use of his attractive wife here as bait . . .

SIR HENRY : His *wife?*

HOLMES : Yes, his wife. He made use of her and of the Hound to kill your uncle and try to kill you. He wanted the Baskerville inheritance for himself.

SIR HENRY : Then . . . who is he? *Was* he?

HOLMES : Your distant cousin, I imagine. He is the very double of your portrait of Sir Hugo.

WATSON : We have Mrs Stapleton to thank for the warnings, Sir Henry.

SIR HENRY : Indeed, I'm grateful, madam. He told me you were away for the night.

BERYL : When I refused to help him bring you to your death tonight he bound and gagged me.

SIR HENRY : And thank you too, Mr Holmes. I guess you were a move ahead all the way.

HOLMES : That is where I prefer to be, especially when dealing with such devilish cunning. The sight of that hound's blazing eyes and flaming jaws will always be with you, I fear, and with the rest of us. Poor brute. It did only what he had trained it for. However, we may now consider the family ghost laid for good. The legend of the Hound of the Baskervilles is at an end.

HOUND : [*A final long, ghostly howl*]

THE EMPTY HOUSE

Characters in order of appearance:

DR WATSON

FIRST MAN

SECOND MAN

THIRD MAN

{ OLD MAN

{ SHERLOCK HOLMES

COLONEL MORAN: (the old Indian army style)

INSPECTOR LESTRADE

CONSTABLE

MRS HUDSON: (motherly; try playing her Scottish)

THE EMPTY HOUSE

[WATSON *introduces the play before the other characters come on stage, when he joins the action*]

WATSON [*narrating*] : It was in the spring of the year 1894 that
all London was interested by the murder of the Honourable Ronald Adair, the son of the Earl of Maynooth,
under the most unusual and inexplicable circumstances.
The youth moved in the best society and had, so far as
was known, no enemies and no particular vices. He was
fond of playing cards, but never for such stakes as would
hurt him. It was shown that after dinner on the evening
of his death he had played a rubber of whist at the
Bagatelle Club with Mr Murray, Sir John Hardy and
Colonel Moran. He returned from the club at ten. His
mother and sister were out for the evening and came
home to the flat at Park Lane at eleven-twenty. Desiring
to say goodnight, Lady Maynooth attempted to enter
her son's room. The door was locked on the inside and
no answer could be got. Help was obtained and the door
forced. The unfortunate young man was lying near the
table. His head had been horribly mutilated by an
expanding revolver bullet, but no weapon was to be
found in the room. On the table lay several piles of gold
coins and a sheet of paper bearing some figures, from
which it was conjectured he had been working out his
losses or winnings at cards.

As I read the evidence at the inquest, which led to a
verdict of wilful murder against some person or persons
unknown, I realised more than ever the loss which the

community had sustained by the death of Sherlock Holmes. There were points about this strange business which I was sure would have appealed to the trained observation and the alert mind of the first criminal agent in Europe. It can be imagined that my close intimacy with Holmes had interested me deeply in crime, and I sometimes even attempted to employ his methods. But on this occasion, standing at about six o'clock in the evening amongst a group of loafers all staring up at a particular window in Park Lane, I confess my train of thought made little progress.

SCENE ONE

[WATSON *stands amongst a street crowd, staring upward*]

1st MAN : I tell yer 'e did 'imself in. Chucked the gun out of the winder as 'e fell to the floor.

2nd MAN : Garn! There's nothin' said abaht no pistol found in Park Lane.

1st MAN : Blimey, mate, you find arf a sovereign in the street, you gonner run an' tell the coppers all abaht it? Some lucky geezer picked that gun up and straight off to the nearest brass balls with it, like any respectable citizen would.

3rd MAN : I say 'is missis done it. It's always their missis wot does it. Shot 'im through the key'ole.

1st MAN : Aw, gor blimey, 'e 'adn't *got* no missis. 'E lived wiv 'is sister and 'is ma. 'Ere, ain't that right, guv'nor?

WATSON : Er, yes, yes. That's right.

1st MAN : There y'are!

3rd MAN : So, what yer bringing 'im into it for? 'Oo asked for your opinion, eh?

WATSON : Opinion? I wasn't stating any opinion. Now, look here, my good man . . . let me past!

> [*He bumps into a tall* OLD MAN *with bushy whiskers, carrying an armful of books; the books fall to the ground*]

OLD MAN : Mind who you are pushing, sir. Those are valuable books.

WATSON : Oh, confound it, I'll pick your blessed books up for you, then. [*He does so*] There. And there. Now, good day to the lot of you!

> [WATSON *exits. The idlers make derisive gestures after him. The* OLD MAN *merely smiles, tucks the books securely under his arm, and follows him*]

SCENE TWO

> [*In the parlour of* WATSON'S *home. He is settling down with the newspaper as his* MAID *enters*]

MAID : Beg pardon, sir.

WATSON : Mm?

MAID : There's a person to see you, sir.

WATSON : In the consulting-room?

MAID : No, here, sir. Won't give his name, but says you'll know him, sir.

WATSON : Oh, does he? Well, tell him . . . No, never mind. I'll see him. Send him in.

MAID : Very good, sir.

> [*She summons in the visitor, who is the* OLD MAN *with the books, which he still carries*]

WATSON : Oh, it's you.

OLD MAN : You're surprised to see me, sir? Tut-tut, I've a conscience, you know. When I chanced to see you come into this house, I thought to myself, 'I'll just step in and tell that kind gentleman that if I was a bit gruff in my manner there was no harm meant, and I was much obliged to him for picking up my books for me.'

WATSON : Well, there was no need at all. It's very civil of you, though. Er, good evening.

OLD MAN : Don't mention it, sir. As a matter of fact, I'm a neighbour of yours—little bookshop at the corner of Church Street. Happy to see you there at any time.

WATSON : Thank you, I . . .

OLD MAN : Maybe you collect yourself, sir?

WATSON : Not really, I . . .

OLD MAN [*showing books*] : *British Birds. Catullus. The Holy War.* A bargain, every one of them. With five volumes you could just fill that gap on your second shelf there.

WATSON [*turning away to look*] : Gap? Oh yes. I see.

> [*The* OLD MAN *is whipping off his whiskers and straightening his back to reveal that he is* HOLMES]

[*Turning back*] But I don't think I . . . *Holmes!*

> [*With a groan,* WATSON *collapses in a faint*]

HOLMES : Dear me! He looked as though he'd seen a ghost. [*Chuckles*] I suppose he had.

[*He takes a brandy flask from his pocket and puts it to* WATSON'S *lips as he assists him*]

WATSON [*weakly*] : Holmes . . .!

HOLMES : Just another sip, my dear fellow. You prescribe it for all your patients, so it should work for you.

WATSON : I can't believe . . .

HOLMES : My dear Watson, I owe you a thousand apologies. I had no idea you would be so affected.

[WATSON *is sitting up again, recovered*]

WATSON : Is . . . is it really you? Is it possible that you succeeded in climbing out of that awful abyss?

[HOLMES *seats himself opposite* WATSON]

HOLMES : I had no serious difficulty in getting out of it, for the very simple reason that I was never in it.

WATSON : Never? But I saw your tracks with my own eyes—yours and Moriarty's. They reached the edge of the path, where you must have struggled. I read your farewell note—I still have it.

HOLMES : The note was absolutely genuine. I had little doubt that I had come to the end of my career when I saw that sinister figure standing on the pathway between me and safety. I read an inexorable purpose in his grey eyes. I exchanged some remarks with him, and obtained his gracious permission to write the short note. When I had done it he rushed at me and threw his long arms round me. He knew that his own game was up and was only anxious to revenge himself on me.

WATSON : Great heavens!

HOLMES : We tottered together on the brink of the fall, but my knowledge of baritsu, the Japanese system of wrestling, proved my salvation. I slipped through his grip. He kicked madly for a few seconds and clawed the air with both his hands. But for all his efforts he could not get his balance, and over he went with a horrible scream. I saw him fall for a long way. Then he struck a rock, bounced off, and splashed into the water.

WATSON : But the tracks. They led only to the edge.

HOLMES : You see, as I stood there on the brink, trying to get back my breath, it came to me in a flash what I must do. I knew that Moriarty was not the only man who had sworn my death. There were at least three others. One or other would almost certainly get me off my guard some day. But if the world was convinced that I was dead, they would drop *their* guard, and sooner or later I could destroy them.

WATSON : I see. But you still haven't told me how you got away from there without leaving a trace.

HOLMES : I examined the rocky wall behind me. In your picturesque account of the matter, which I read with great interest some months later, you assert that the wall was sheer. That was not literally true. A few small footholds presented themselves. It was not a pleasant climb, Watson, with the fall roaring beneath me and Moriarty's scream still in my ears. One mistake would have been fatal. But I struggled upward and at long last reached safety.

WATSON : That was *three years* ago, Holmes. You have never been in touch with me until now.

HOLMES : I owe you an apology for that. It was vital that I should be thought dead, and you would not have written half so convincing an account of my end, had you known otherwise. Brilliant, my dear fellow! I was gripped by every sentence of it.

WATSON [*chuckling*] : Well, it's a remarkable business, and this is the happiest day of my life. But where have you been all this time?

HOLMES : Oh, I have not been idle. I was unable to come back to London, where I am too well known. I travelled for two years in Tibet, where I spent some days with the head lama. You may have read of the explorations of a Norwegian named Sigerson?

WATSON : Certainly I did. Holmes, you don't tell me *you* were . . .

HOLMES : None other. I looked in at Mecca and paid an interesting visit to the Khalifa at Khartoum. Then I moved on to France, where I spent some months doing research into the coal-tar derivatives in a laboratory at Montpellier. It was there I learned that only one of my principal enemies was left in London. I was preparing to return and deal with him when this Park Lane business hastened my movements.

WATSON : The Adair murder? What has that to do with you?

HOLMES : You will find that out tonight, if you are game for another adventure in our old manner.

WATSON [*rubbing his hands*] : I'll say so, Holmes. The good old times, which I believed were past for ever!

HOLMES : There will be danger.

WATSON : All the better. Where will it take us?

HOLMES : To our former abode, 221B Baker Street, where, incidentally, I called this afternoon and induced near hysterics in Mrs Hudson.

WATSON : [*Laughs*]

HOLMES : Or rather, our precise destination will be the house immediately across the street. I was delighted to find that it is empty, which suits my purposes perfectly.

WATSON : What are we going to do there, Holmes?

HOLMES : If I'm not mistaken, we shall be meeting someone. Have you a *Who's Who?*

WATSON [*getting up*] : Last year's edition. Will that do?

HOLMES : Admirably.

> [WATSON *brings him the volume.* HOLMES *seeks out an entry*]

Listen to this, Watson. [*Reads*] 'Moran, Sebastian.' Does the name mean anything to you?

WATSON : I don't think so.

HOLMES : Well, well, such is fame. But I remember you had never heard of the late Professor James Moriarty. Care to read up Moran for yourself?

> [*He passes the book to* WATSON, *who reads aloud*]

WATSON [*reading*] : 'Moran, Sebastian, Colonel. Formerly First Bangalore Pioneers. Born London, 1840, son of Sir Augustus Moran, C.B., once British Minister to Persia. Educated Eton and Oxford. Served in Jowaki Campaign, Afghan Campaign (mentioned in despatches), Sherpur and Cabul. Author of *Heavy Game in the Western Himalayas*, 1881, *Three Months in the Jungle*, 1884. Clubs: Anglo-Indian, Tankerville, Bagatelle Card Club.' Bagatelle? That's where young Adair had been that evening he was murdered.

HOLMES : Just so. A pretty impressive record, Colonel Moran's, wouldn't you agree?

WATSON : Oh, yes. I never chanced to meet him in my own service in Afghanistan.

HOLMES : I believe the story is still told in India of how he crawled down a drain after a wounded man-eating tiger.

WATSON : Ah, that fellow! A brave man.

HOLMES : He did honourably enough in his day. There are some trees, Watson, which grow to a certain height, and then suddenly develop some unsightly eccentricity. You will see it often in humans, too. I have a theory that the individual represents in his development the whole procession of his ancestors, and that such a sudden turn to good or evil stands for some strong influence which came into the line of his pedigree.

WATSON : That sounds rather fanciful, Holmes.

HOLMES : Well, I don't insist upon it. Whatever the cause, though, Colonel Moran began to go wrong. Without any open scandal, he made India too hot to hold him. He retired to London, and such was his reputation that Moriarty sought him out.

WATSON : Aha! Now we're getting to it.

HOLMES : Moriarty supplied him liberally with money and used him in only one or two very high-class jobs, which no ordinary criminal could have undertaken.

WATSON : He's a criminal, then.

HOLMES : He is more than that. When Moriarty was alive Colonel Moran was his chief of staff. He was the second most dangerous man in London. Now he's the first. He was so cleverly covered in everything he did that when the Moriarty gang was broken up there was nothing to incriminate him.

WATSON : Holmes, is this the person you expect we shall meet in Baker Street this evening?

HOLMES : Suffice it to say that he is the one man remaining who would wish to assassinate me the moment he gets the opportunity. For my part, I have been waiting these three years for an opportunity of laying him by the heels. I have a piece of work for us both tonight which, if we can bring it to a successful conclusion, will in itself justify a man's life on this planet. Now, my dear chap, we shall have time for a mouthful of dinner before we go, if you will be so kind, then we will take a cab to somewhere about Cavendish Square and go from there by foot.

There are plenty of small lanes and mews, which is as well. I am not ready to be generally recognised yet.

WATSON : But I thought they supposed you dead.

HOLMES : As I climbed from that abyss, a huge rock, falling from above, boomed past me. For an instant I thought it was an accident, but a moment later I saw a man's head against the darkening sky. Moriarty had not been there alone. A confederate—and even that one glance told me who he was—had witnessed my escape from death. I eluded him on that occasion, but I knew he would keep constant watch for my return to London. Despite my disguise, his sentinel saw me enter 221B this afternoon.

WATSON : How d'you know?

HOLMES : I recognised him, a harmless enough fellow named Parker, garrotter by trade, and a remarkable performer on the jew's-harp.

WATSON [laughing joyously] : The same old Holmes!

SCENE THREE

[In the empty house in Baker Street, with the lighted windows of 221B visible opposite. HOLMES and WATSON enter stealthily]

WATSON [low] : Surely that is Baker Street.

HOLMES : Exactly. We are in Camden House, which stands opposite our own old quarters and commands an excellent view of that picturesque pile. Might I trouble you, Watson, to draw a little nearer to the window, taking every precaution not to show yourself.

WATSON : Very well.

HOLMES : Now look at our old rooms—the starting-point of so many of your little fairy-tales. We will see if my three years of absence have taken away my power to surprise you.

WATSON : Good . . . good heavens! Your silhouette up there against the window. It's . . . it's marvellous!

HOLMES : I trust that age doth not wither nor custom stale my infinite variety. It really *is* rather like me, isn't it?

WATSON : I'd swear it was you.

HOLMES : The credit belongs to Monsieur Oscar Meunier, of Grenoble. It is a bust in wax. He spent some days in doing the moulding. The rest I arranged myself during my visit to 221B this afternoon. You see, I have the strongest possible motives for wishing certain people to think I am idling indoors when I am really elsewhere.

WATSON : Holmes, the silhouette is all very fine, but surely thay have only to keep their eyes on it for long enough to see that it never moves.

HOLMES : Have you been keeping *your* eyes on it?

WATSON : Yes, I have.

HOLMES : Then, pray do so for a little longer.

WATSON : I really don't see . . . Bless my soul! It . . . it moved. Just then.

HOLMES : Of course it has moved. Am I such a farcical bungler that I'd erect an obvious dummy in a way that no one would be taken in by it?

WATSON : Then . . .

HOLMES : Ssh! [*Low*] Someone is coming. Quick, Watson. Quickly and quietly, away from the window and into that alcove in the shadows.

> [*They tiptoe into an alcove removed from the pool of faint light. In a moment* COLONEL MORAN *enters the*

> *room. He produces the separate barrel and stock of an*
> *air rifle, which he assembles, and screws on a tele-*
> *scopic night-sight. He goes to the window and quietly*
> *raises the sash a few inches. He kneels in a firing*
> *position, takes very careful aim at the silhouette, and*
> *fires. There is a distant crash of breaking glass*]

MORAN : And that's the end of you at last, Mr Sherlock Holmes!

> [HOLMES *comes out of the shadows*]

HOLMES : Oh, no, Colonel Moran . . .

MORAN [*spinning round*] : Ah!

HOLMES : Sherlock Holmes is still here. Hold on to him, Watson.

> [WATSON *leaps out and grabs* MORAN *before he can*
> *stand up. He wrestles the gun from his hands.*
> HOLMES *blows three long blasts on a police whistle.*
> *Men's voices are heard and* INSPECTOR LESTRADE
> *and a* CONSTABLE *run in. The* CONSTABLE *seizes*
> MORAN]

LESTRADE : Got him, Larkin?

CONSTABLE : Yes, sir. [*Handcuffing* MORAN] He'll come quiet now.

HOLMES : Good work, Lestrade. I thought you needed a little help, so I came back from the dead to provide it.

LESTRADE : We got your message at the Yard, sir, and I asked to be put on this case myself. It's good to see you back from wherever you've been, Mr Holmes. And to see you again, Doctor.

WATSON : The pleasure's all mine tonight, Lestrade.

MORAN : You fiend, Holmes! You cunning, cunning fiend!

HOLMES : One of us is not so pleased, perhaps because I haven't introduced him. Gentlemen, Colonel Sebastian Moran, once of Her Majesty's Indian Army, and the

best heavy-game shot our Eastern Empire has ever pro-
duced. Well, Colonel, 'Journeys end in lovers' meet-
ings,' as the old play says. I don't think I have had the
pleasure of seeing you since you favoured me with your
attentions at the Reichenbach Falls.

MORAN : Swine!

HOLMES : I believe I am correct, Colonel, in saying that your
bag of tigers remains unrivalled? That makes me wonder
that my very simple stratagem should deceive so old a
shikari. Haven't you tethered a kid, lain above it with
your rifle, and waited for the bait to attract your tiger?
Well, Colonel, this empty house is my tree, and you are
my tiger.

MORAN [*to* LESTRADE] : You—Inspector or whatever you
are—you may or may not have cause for arresting me,
but there can be no reason why I should be exposed to
the gibes of this person. If I am in the hands of the law,
let things be done in a legal way.

LESTRADE : Well, that's reasonable enough. Colonel Sebastian
Moran, I must caution you that anything you say . . .

HOLMES : One moment, Lestrade. Might I ask what charge
you intend to prefer?

LESTRADE : Charge? Why, the attempted murder of Mr Sherlock Holmes.

HOLMES : Not so. I do not propose to appear in the matter at
all. To you, and to you only, belongs the credit for the
remarkable arrest you have effected. Lestrade, I con-
gratulate you. With your usual happy mixture of cunning and audacity, you have got him.

WATSON : Got him? Got who, Holmes?

HOLMES : The man the whole force has been seeking in
vain—the man who shot the Honourable Ronald Adair
with an expanding bullet from an air-rifle through the

window of the second-floor flat of No. 427 Park Lane.

[*Astonished reactions from* ALL. HOLMES *calmly picks up the weapon and examines it*]

That's your charge, Lestrade. You will need this as evidence, and I will return it shortly, with your permission. Watson, if you can endure the draught from a broken window, I think that half an hour in my study over a cigar may afford you some profitable amusement.

[WATSON *and* LESTRADE *exchange wondering glances behind* HOLMES'S *back as he strides out, carrying the gun. The* CONSTABLE *gives* MORAN'S *arm a jerk and guides him off, snarling.* WATSON *follows.* LESTRADE *looks around the room, scratches his head, and follows*]

SCENE FOUR

[*The parlour of 221B Baker Street.* MRS HUDSON *is on hands and knees, using a dustpan and brush to sweep up broken glass from under the window, before which, on a table, stands the head and shoulders bust of* HOLMES, *with a bullet-hole in its forehead.* HOLMES *and* WATSON *enter*]

HOLMES : Never mind a bit of broken glass, Mrs Hudson. I hope you observed all precautions yourself.

MRS HUDSON [*still sweeping*] : I did just as you told me, Mr Holmes. Why, it's Doctor Watson again!

WATSON : A pleasure to see you once more, Mrs Hudson.

HOLMES : The good doctor can't make out how the dummy managed to move about every now and then. Perhaps you will enlighten him.

[MRS HUDSON *moves on her knees to the table. Keeping her head well down, she reaches up and shifts the bust to and fro with her hand*]

WATSON [*laughing*] : So that was it!

MRS HUDSON [*getting up*] : Mind you, I got a bit of a fright when that bullet came through the window. It's spoilt that beautiful wax figure of you, Mr Holmes. Passed right through it and flattened itself against the wall.

[*She picks the bullet off the table and hands it to* HOLMES]

I picked it up from the carpet.

HOLMES : A soft revolver bullet, as you perceive, Watson.

WATSON [*puzzled*] : Revolver? Yes, indeed!

HOLMES : All right, Mrs Hudson. I'm much obliged for your assistance.

MRS HUDSON : Thank you, sir.

[*She exits*]

HOLMES : Now, Watson, let me see you in your old seat once more.

[WATSON *takes off his coat and and occupies his old chair in state.* HOLMES *beams, throws off his coat and jacket, and dons his old dressing gown from behind the door*]

WATSON : But, Holmes, a *revolver* bullet?

[HOLMES *picks up the air-rifle and hands it to him to examine*]

HOLMES : An admirable and unique weapon. Noiseless, and of tremendous power. I knew Von Herder, the blind German mechanic who constructed it to the order of the late Professor Moriarty. For years I have been aware of its existence, though I've never before had the opportunity of handling it.

WATSON : An air-gun adapted to fire revolver bullets!

HOLMES : There's genius in that, Watson. Who would suspect any such thing? Noiseless, yet deadly in the hands of one of the best shots in the world.

WATSON : Then this is the same weapon which killed young Adair?

HOLMES : Without doubt.

WATSON : And it was Moran who used it?

HOLMES : Remember the names of those who had been playing cards with Adair that evening at the Bagatelle Club—Mr Murray, Sir John Hardy, *Colonel Moran*.

WATSON : Ah! But *murder?*

[HOLMES *commences blandly to light his pipe*]

HOLMES : Here we come into those realms of conjecture, where the most logical mind may be at fault. Each may form his own hypothesis upon the present evidence, and yours is as likely to be correct as mine.

WATSON : I, er . . . I haven't exactly decided upon mine, Holmes.

HOLMES : Well, for what it is worth, here is my own guess. Moran undoubtedly played foul at cards—of that I have been long aware. I believe that on the day of the murder Adair had discovered him cheating. It is scarcely likely that a youngster would make a hideous scandal by exposing a well-known man so much older than himself. Probably he spoke to Moran privately, threatening to expose him unless he voluntarily resigned his membership of the club and promised not to play cards again. Such exclusion would ruin Moran, who lived by his ill-gotten card-gains. He therefore murdered Adair with a crack shot from a weapon none would suspect. How is that? Will it pass?

WATSON [*chuckling*] : No doubt you're as right as ever you
were, Holmes.

HOLMES : It will be verified or disproved at the trial.

> [*He takes the weapon from* WATSON, *puts it to his
> shoulder, and takes aim at the bust of himself.* WAT-
> SON *looks apprehensive.* HOLMES *pulls the trigger,
> but the breach is empty. He props the gun up against
> the fireplace and proceeds to light his pipe*]

Meanwhile, my dear Watson, Colonel Moran will trouble us no more. The famous air-gun of Von Herder will
embellish the Scotland Yard museum. And, once again,
Mr Sherlock Holmes is free to devote his life to explain-
ing those interesting little problems which the complex
life of London so plentifully presents.

OTHER PLAYS BY MICHAEL AND MOLLIE HARDWICK

Four Sherlock Holmes Plays

Plays based on *The Blue Carbuncle*, *The Mazarin Stone*, *Charles Augustus Milverton* and *The Speckled Band*.

The Game's Afoot

One-act versions of four Sherlock Holmes stories:
The Three Garridebs, *The Reigate Squires*, *Black Peter* and *The Dying Detective*.

Four More Sherlock Holmes Plays

This volume contains: *The Norwood Builder*, *The Disappearance of Lady Francis Carfax*, *Shoscombe Old Place*, *The Illustrious Client*.

Plays from Dickens

Five of the most notable scenes from the novels, four dramatised as ten-minute classroom plays and one as a longer play suitable for public performance.